Greatest Moments in Ohio State Football History

TRIUMPH
B O O K S
CHICAGO

RESEARCH ASSISTANCE

Ohio State University Archives, Ohio State University Sports Information, Roy Hewitt and *The Plain Dealer* Sports Department, Jerry Hoegner, Gloria Gamble, Jim Russ, Terry Jacoby, Susan Kordalski, the Rose Bowl Media Relations Office, the Fiesta Bowl Media Relations Office, Chance Brockway, Wide World Photos, Bettmann Archives and Allsport Photography USA.

Contributing Writers
Bruce Hooley: Pages 1–9, 35–39, 113–17, 125–29, 154–58, 160–86, 188–93, 197–203
John Dietrich: Pages 16–27, 32–33, 40–62, 64–73
Tom Place: Pages 74–75
Ed Chay: Pages 76–98, 100–111, 118–23, 130–37
Hal Lebovitz: Page 99
Dwayne Cheeks: Pages 139–40, 142–44, 146–48
Thom Greer: Pages 141, 145
Bob Dolgan: Page 149
Burt Graeff: Pages 151–53
Bud Shaw: Page 169
Bill Livingston: Pages 187, 194–95
Todd Porter: Pages 204–14

Library of Congress Cataloging-in-Publication Data available upon request.

This book is available in quantity at special discounts for your group or organization. For further information, contact:
Triumph Books
601 South LaSalle Street
Suite 500
Chicago, Illinois 60605
(312) 939-3330
Fax (312) 663-3557

Printed in China
ISBN 1-57243-578-X
Design by Daniel J. Janke

The photos on pages 204–14 courtesy of AP/Wide World Photos.

CONTENTS

FOREWORD

By Archie Griffin

When I looked up and scanned the seats in Sun Devil Stadium on that balmy desert night in 2003, I thought it would be a magical evening for Ohio State University and its football program. When fireworks lit up the star-filled sky and scarlet and gray confetti shot from the ground and fluttered down like a thousand Buckeye butterflies, I was certain of it.

It was the same kind of certainty I had when we hired Jim Tressel as football coach in 2001. I could see his character, his personality, his integrity, the way he shapes young men's lives—not only on the football field but, more importantly, off it—and I knew we had found the right man to lead our team, our community and our fans to where they want to be. The naysayers didn't believe a coach from Division I-AA could lead a major college football team, but the fact that he had led Youngstown State to several national titles was something we viewed very positively. He knew how to get to the championship game, and he knew how to win there. I have believed from the beginning that he is a winner. After the six weeks he had to prepare for Miami, I was totally confident that the Buckeyes were in great hands.

On January 3, 2003—a night I will never forget—the Buckeye nation was well represented at the Fiesta Bowl. You looked around the stadium and saw nothing but scarlet and gray. You saw very little Miami Hurricanes green and orange. I shouldn't have been surprised by the effort our fans made to be there. We had 16,000 tickets to sell, but somehow, some way, our fans managed to get more. I was blown away by how loyal our Ohio State fans are.

That game was the high point of my long association with Ohio State, including my two Heisman Trophy-winning seasons. It was the end of a 34-year span without a national championship.

The groundwork for our Fiesta Bowl started during the previous January, when Mike Doss made his decision to stay at Ohio State. The impact coach Tressel was having on his players was obvious then, as it is now. Doss set an example for future Buckeyes when he made the decision to stay in school.

I thought something special was in the offing after the Purdue game. That's when I began to believe that a national title could be in the cards.

The way we won that game—with a touchdown pass on fourth-and-one with less than two minutes left in the game—was like destiny.

Very few people thought this team had a chance of winning the national championship. But they refused to lose. They weren't a team that ran away with games—quite the contrary. They won seven games by seven points or less to get to the Fiesta Bowl. They were a team that won tough games. They were persistent and consistent. They just got the job done.

At the end of the night, when all the Buckeye butterflies had floated to the ground, after coach Tressel accepted the national championship trophy, I was left with one thought: Ohio State is a special place because of special people. It has been led by extraordinary individuals throughout its history. To try to boil down what makes us special in the pages of a book is nearly impossible, but this volume has done a great job in doing so. In the coming pages, you will read about some of those wonderful folks who made us what we are, and about what they have done for football—something that is in our blood in this great state.

OSU History Is Filled With Legends, Tradition and Indelible Memories

T his is what they tell you at freshman orientation, before you ever take a class at Ohio State University.

Sorry, make that, The Ohio State University.

They make a point of telling you that, too.

"It's The Ohio State University, pal, and don't you forget it.

"Not an Ohio State University or even just plain old Ohio State University. It's THE Ohio State University," as in, The One and Only, Biggest, Baddest and Best Ohio State University.

That's important.

But it's not the last thing they tell you.

That stuff about the buses leaving for West Campus every 15 minutes and Orton Hall housing the chimes and Mirror Lake being a wonderful place to spend a spring day and, oh, yeah, don't ever let anyone sell you a subscription to the Lantern because it's free, stupid ... all that stuff is important.

But all that information is provided before a guy walks on stage in front of an auditorium full of freshmen-to-be, just before dismissing them to their hometowns for the rest of the last summer of their pre-college lives.

Slowly, he pulls something out of his pocket and holds it between his thumb and forefinger.

"This," he says, serious as an IRS audit, "is a buckeye.

"A buckeye," he continues, "is a nut.

"A poisonous nut.

"If you eat this nut," he adds, pausing for high drama, "you will die.

"So, you see," he finishes, a trace of a smile leaking out the corners of his lips, "you are about to attend the only school in the country named after a killer nut."

Oh, there are legions of Lions and Tigers and Bears, but there are, indeed, no other Buckeyes in the land.

No copy.

No imitation.

No substitute.

No generic to blur the edges, muddle the middle or cheapen the authenticity of the original.

When Woody Hayes wanted to seal the deal with

In 1975, running back Archie Griffin (45) became the first player ever to win the Heisman Trophy twice.

On Oct. 21, 1922, 71,385 attended the dedication game at Ohio Stadium against – who else – Michigan.

a recruit, he'd tilt his head a little to the side, adjust those horn-rimmed glasses and give the kid a little fatherly thump on the shoulder.

Then he'd say, "Son, you're going to be a Buckeye."

And all the kid could offer in return was, "Where do I sign?"

To be a Buckeye is to be a little stubborn, a little arrogant and a little nuts.

A little killer nuts.

That's a Buckeye.

Nowhere is that craziness more evident than when Buckeyes the world over gather in body, mind and spirit at their shrine aside the Olentangy.

It's there in Ohio Stadium where more than mere diversion takes place.

Football Saturdays in the mammoth, double-decked Horseshoe are the truest representation of the collegiality that binds Buckeyes from bygone eras to those of the present and future.

It is the one event that bridges the canyon separating the members of the largest alumni association in America from those who never quite made it through that lamentable 20-hour foreign language requirement and those who never even strolled across the Oval.

No, sir, it doesn't take a diploma to appreciate and love Ohio State football.

All it takes is a reverence for tradition and a thirst to drink it down in massive doses.

Who else has the Victory Bell, Script Ohio and the fifth-quarter field goal?

From 1972 to 1974, Ohio State played Southern Cal in three straight Rose Bowls. The Buckeyes lost two of the three, winning after the 1973 season.

Who else has the Snow Bowl, Senior Tackle and the Captain's Breakfast?

Who else has Buckeye Grove, Buckeye leaves and the Buckeye Battle Cry?

Who else has skull sessions, the ramp entrance and Hang On Sloopy?

No one, that's who.

Who else could see the beauty in the bite-sized logic of three yards and a cloud of dust?

Who else could overlook the simplicity and warm to the wisdom of this warning, "Three things can happen when you pass, and two of them are bad"?

Who else could make a battle call from the simple observation, "They put their pants on just like we do"?

Only Buckeyes, that's who.

From Ohio Field to Ohio Stadium, from John Wilce to John Cooper, OSU football has thrilled generations and berthed indelible memories in the minds of those who bleed scarlet and gray.

Of course, you cannot bleed without the occasional cut, and any Buckeye can attest that there have been ample wounds to temper the triumphs.

Do not come hungry to any tailgate parties, Randy Vataha, Levi Jackson, Sam (Bam) Cunningham, Shelton Diggs, Wally Henry, Charles White, John Kolesar or Tshimanga Biakabutuka.

You either, Charlie Bauman.

All of you have done enough.

But while the intrusions of those adversaries upon OSU's achievements cannot be forgotten or forgiven, neither can they obscure the many proud moments in a football legacy about to begin its 114th season.

4

Five national championships from one set of voters or another, six Rose Bowl victories and 28 Big Ten titles or co-titles provide a pretty good elixir to chase away the blues.

Particularly the maize-and-blues.

Just as Ali had Frazier and Leonard had Hearns, Ohio State's ascendancy to the upper echelon of college football greatness has been alternately constructed and occasionally compromised by its association with arch-rival Michigan.

About the only thing the two schools agree on is that their annual, late-November border war ranks as the No.1 rivalry in college football.

Auburn and Alabama might debate that, as would Tennessee and Florida, Army and Navy, Texas and Oklahoma or UCLA and Southern Cal, but all protests ring hollow to anyone who's witnessed an OSU-Michigan game.

Within that series lurks a motherlode of memories that time cannot erase.

There was Les Horvath, leading the Buckeyes back from a 14-12 deficit in the final eight minutes in 1944.

"We're not going to pass. We're not going to fumble. We're going to score," Horvath told his teammates in the huddle before following through with the 2-yard run that gave OSU the victory and himself the Heisman Trophy.

There was the goal-line stand and 99-yard, go-ahead drive in 1954, the first time a Michigan win saved Hayes' hide.

There was Woody, trashing a yard-maker when Thom Darden went over the back (oh, yes, he did) in 1971 and no flag fell.

And don't forget Tom Klaban's four field goals, Ray Griffin's interception, Jim Laughlin's punt block, Vaughn Broadnax clearing Art Schlichter's path to the end zone, Earle Bruce in a fedora and those hell-raising "EARLE" headbands on his players.

Still not convinced?

Then go ask the 50,503 who sat through Ohio's worst blizzard in 37 years for the 1950 Snow Bowl at the Horseshoe.

Start with five inches on the ground at kickoff,

Ohio State has waved the flag as National Champions in 1942 (9-1 record), 1954 (10-0), 1957 (9-1), 1961 (8-0-1), 1968 (10-0) and 2002 (14-0).

Ohio State's 10-0 season in 1954 included a 21-7 victory over Michigan (above), which featured 14 fourth-quarter points for the Buckeyes.

with eight more falling throughout, and 28 mph winds whipping the white stuff into players' eyes like little ice-covered darts.

Michigan won that installment, 9-3, without so much as a single first down, and 14 days later Ohio State coach Wes Fesler resigned because of "the tension brought about by the tremendous desire to win football games."

Fesler had been a three-time All-American at OSU in the late 1920s, bridging the gap between OSU's first All-American, Chic Harley, and its first

national championship under Coach Paul Brown in 1942.

But forgiveness has always had its limits at Ohio State, and losing to Michigan has always been beyond those borders.

"You can have a good season if you win the rest of your games," Cooper is fond of saying. "But you can't have a great season unless you beat Michigan."

The great seasons at OSU began with Harley, who played in only one losing game and was its first of six three-time All-Americans in 1916, 1917 and 1919.

Those first two years marked the initial Western Conference (later to become Big Ten) championships

OSU would win, including the remarkable 1917 season in which the Buckeyes outscored their opposition by an aggregate 292-6.

Harley's passing, punting, running and drop-kicking was so electrifying, demand for tickets forced the university to abandon 10,000-seat Ohio Field and plan the construction of a new stadium that would seat — gulp — 66,210 and cost — gulp, gulp — more than $1 million.

Those who labeled Athletic Director Lynn W. St. John crazy to commit to such a structure ate their words when, 14 months after ground was broken, the Horseshoe welcomed an overflow crowd of 71,385 for the 1922 game against Michigan.

There's that name again.

For a long time, too, the Wolverines dominated the series that began in 1897.

Ohio State didn't score on its arch rival until the sixth game between the teams, didn't win until the 16th installment and didn't start evening things up until Francis "Close the Gates of Mercy" Schmidt arrived as coach in 1934.

It was Schmidt who told his players, "Michigan puts its pants on just like we do," then went out and proved it by beating the Wolverines four straight times.

Ever since, each OSU player on a team that beats Michigan comes away from the season with a tiny pant-shaped, gold pendant to commemorate the triumph.

Two other hallowed traditions sandwich The Game each year, starting with Senior Tackle the Friday before kickoff.

One by one, OSU's seniors line up for one final

Carroll C. Widdoes (top) and Wesley E. Fesler all share important parts in Ohio State football history.

blast at the blocking sled, then stand before a crowd of 20,000 as some luminary from the past waxes about the rivalry.

The Captains Breakfast the morning after Michigan is a private affair, reserved only for those elected to lead their respective Ohio State teams.

"When you're in that room, surrounded by all those guys who've played here in the past, that's when it really brings home the tradition of what it means to play here," said 1996 OSU captain Greg Bellisari. "The guys in that room share a special bond."

Not all those guys will wind up in Buckeye Grove, the wooded area outside Ohio Stadium's south end zone, where a buckeye tree has been planted in honor of every All-American, all 75 of them, since 1914.

John Stungis isn't honored there, but his immortality in OSU lore is secure.

It was Stungis, one of Paul Brown's Baby Buckeyes on the war-depleted 1943 roster, who kicked the "fifth-quarter" field goal that defeated Illinois, 29-26, in the penultimate game of that season.

An offsides penalty on the Illini on the game's final play nearly went undetected, causing both teams to depart for their locker rooms and half the Ohio Stadium crowd to depart.

But Brown, given the option to decline the penal-

Paul Warfield was an outstanding halfback at OSU and an All-Pro receiver in the NFL.

ty and take the tie, risk victory on OSU's first field goal of the season or, quite possibly, suffer defeat on a blocked kick returned the other way, gambled.

"I never missed one of these myself, Johnny," Brown told Stungis on the way back to the field.

"No kidding, coach? How many have you made?"

"I never tried one," Brown laughed, breaking the tension just enough for Stungis to relax and deliver the game-winner.

Not all last-second kicks have gone the Buckeyes' way, of course. But, thankfully, there's been a counterbalance for every disappointment.

As much as it hurt when Uwe von Schamann hit his deciding field goal in Oklahoma's pulsating 29-28 triumph over the Buckeyes in 1977, it didn't hurt as bad as it felt good three years earlier when Michigan's Mike Lantry missed from 30 yards with 18 seconds left to preserve OSU's 12-10 victory and third straight Rose Bowl trip.

The jubilant shouts of Tom Hamlin — "He missed it! He missed it! He missed it! — still waft melodiously in the memory banks of those who stood poised over their rakes while leaf-gathering took a time out for the fourth of five straight OSU-Michigan games decided by a touchdown or less.

Those nail-biters typify the intensity of the rivalry, which over a 59-game span from 1927-85 saw each team score exactly 800 points and OSU edge to a 29-27-3 advantage.

Examine a slightly different era and the story is still the same, for from 1948-91 the count stood 21 wins for Michigan, 21 for OSU and a pair of ties.

Clearly, big wins don't come often, so when they do, they are sweet.

That 50-20 OSU win over Michigan in 1961 came thanks in part to a certain Hayes assistant coach who called every single play.

Some guy named Schembechler, who had the good sense to hand the football quite frequently to Buckeye fullback Bob Ferguson in his last college game.

Ferguson powered for four touchdowns to give Ohio State its highest scoring total ever against the Wolverines.

Then, on his way to the locker room, Ferguson obliged a young fan's request for the chin strap off his helmet as a souvenir.

Now flash forward seven years, to 1968, and a pep rally the night before a Rose Bowl-deciding showdown between OSU and – who else? – Michigan.

That same fan, clutching that same chin strap, approaches Ohio State fullback Jim Otis and bestows the piece of history upon him as a good luck charm.

Otis tapes it underneath his shoulder pads the next afternoon and, like Ferguson, scores four touchdowns against the Wolverines in a 50-14 OSU victory.

The margin of that drubbing would ultimately lead to Schembechler, gone by now to Miami of Ohio, being named the following season as Michigan's head coach.

It also led another coaching legend in waiting to approach Hayes afterward, wanting to know why The Old Man opted to round off the triumph with a rub-their-noses-in-it, two-point conversion after the Buckeyes' final touchdown.

"Coach," then-OSU defensive backfield assistant Lou Holtz asked Hayes, "why did you go for two?"

"Because," Hayes smirked, "they wouldn't let me go for three."

That's killer.

That's nuts.

That's a Buckeye.

THE
MAGIC
AND THE
MEMORIES

HARLEY ZIG-ZAGS OSU TO WIN WESTERN TITLE

Ohio State won the Western Conference championship by defeating its only rival, Northwestern, in the final game of the season, 23-3. It completed a 7-0 season for OSU.

Though OSU showed greater strength throughout the first three periods, the game was undecided until the final period. With the third quarter over, Ohio State led only 3-0.

After Northwestern tied it on a 37-yard field goal, Charles Harley put OSU ahead to stay with a zig-zagging, 64-yard run for a touchdown.

Columbus, Nov. 25, 1916						
Northwestern	0	0	0	3	–	3
Ohio State	0	0	3	20	–	23

With the score tied at 3, Chic Harley put Ohio State ahead to stay with a 64-yard touchdown run in the fourth quarter.

After that the scarlet and gray started an irresistible rush that Northwestern could not stop.

Time after time the Ohio State backs ripped through positions that, heretofore, had been difficult ones to pass. Richard Boesel was the star at this, making four consecutive first downs in as many plays just off tackle.

Ohio State's second touchdown came after a Northwestern fumble, which was recovered by Ferdinand Holtkamp on the Wildcat 20 following a Harley punt.

After a 1-yard gain by Boesel, Harley twisted and slashed through the purple defense for another thrilling touchdown run.

Charles (Chic) Harley passed, kicked and ran his way onto the All-America teams of 1916, 1917 and 1919.

With five minutes to play, Harley received a punt and carried it to the 30-yard line before he was tackled.

On the next play, Harley made a 10-yard toss to Clarence MacDonald, and MacDonald carried to the Northwestern 3. Frank Sorenson ran in for the TD from there.

While Ohio State did not win the contest until the last quarter, the superiority of the scarlet and gray could scarcely have been questioned at any time.

Only in passing did the visitors excel, and there was comparatively little of that style of play.

Ohio State tried but six passes, completing four of them for a total of 31 yards, while the visitors made six of their 18 good for 88 yards.

Rushing the ball was where OSU shone brightest. For every first down made by Northwestern, OSU had nearly two, the purple forcing the linemen to move the sticks nine times while Ohio made its count 17. Of the ground gained, OSU made 300 yards to Northwestern's 181 – 172 of Ohio State's coming in the last period.

OSU ENDS MICHIGAN JINX TO WIN WESTERN CONFERENCE TITLE

O hio State celebrated the burial rites for the Michigan jinx. Led by the sensational play of Chic Harley, famous All-American halfback, the great Buckeye machine triumphed over Michigan, 13-3.

Conclusively and sensationally, after 22

Ann Arbor, Mich., Oct. 25, 1919					
Ohio State	7	0	6	0	– 13
Michigan	0	3	0	0	– 3

years of defeat, the Buckeyes celebrated their supremacy over the Wolverines. The play of the OSU line far surpassed that of Michigan's.

BUCKEYES VS. MICHIGAN, 1919

The maize and blue backs were unable to gain except at infrequent intervals.

Just after the start of the third quarter, with the score 7-3 Ohio State, Harley slipped at least three tacklers and dashed for an impressive 50-yard touchdown from punt formation.

The kick failed, leading to the final score of 13-3.

Harley's TD was set up by a 17-yard run by Pete Stinchcomb on a quarterback sneak.

The scarlet and gray registered its first touchdown when left tackle Iolas Huffman broke through

Ohio State quarterback Pete Stinchcomb set up the Buckeyes' second touchdown with a 17-yard run.

the line and blocked a punt. The ball rolled over the goal line and right end Jim Flower pounced on it for the score.

It was not the fault of Cliff Sparks, Fielding Yost's nifty quarterback, that the Buckeyes finally achieved their ambition of defeating Michigan. Sparks was the only man who could gain at all on OSU. It was he who kicked a field goal from the 43-yard line in the second period that resulted in Michigan's only score.

Coach K.W. Wilce began to use strategy here.

He sent in several substitutes while Stinchcomb did everything to stall the team. Stinchcomb called signals of five strings each and the Michigan crowd hooted, but realized that nothing could be done to help it.

Yost sought to counteract the OSU strategy by resorting to forward passes. Michigan tried 18 tosses during the game, but none were successful. Harley, Stinchcomb and Thomas Davies were outstanding in the defensive backfield.

Fully 25,000 persons attended the game today, one-fifth of these being OSU fans.

Before the start of the game, the Michigan band, garbed in the regimental uniform of blue with yellow streamers, paraded up and down the field. Shortly after, the Ohio State band, clad in khaki of the R.O.T.C., marched on.

Between the halves, a collection for the Roosevelt memorial fund was taken up, the crowd tossing silver into two big American flags that were stretched out in front of the bleachers. Close to $4,000 was raised.

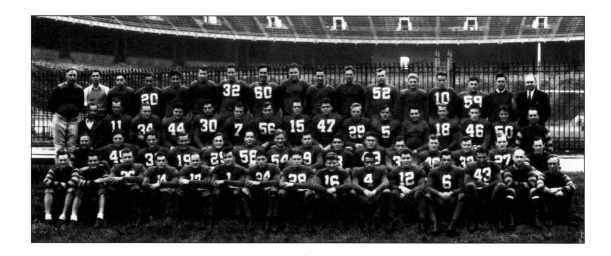

OHIO STATE CIRCUS PARADES THROUGH FEEBLE MICHIGAN

Columbus, Nov. 17, 1934						
Michigan	0	0	0	0	—	0
Ohio State	0	7	7	20	—	34

This was the end of the rainbow.

A scarlet and gray rainbow.

Before a vast host of 68,678 spectators, who rubbed their eyes and peered down from the heights wondering if it could be true, Ohio State today finally brought Michigan to judgment.

The score was 34-0. With five touchdowns, with lateral and forward passes and crushing power, the aroused and inspired Scarlet Buckeyes of High Street today wrought that long delayed vengeance upon their ancient enemy.

The game is over now, and down in the huge pit of the stadium, the scarlet and gray-wrapped goal posts are toppling — for the first time in history.

A laughing and deliriously jubilant mass of humanity, the biggest crowd in Ohio Stadium since 1928, stands around cheering as the goal posts fall, are crushed and twisted to bits, and are carried away on a hysterical wave of ecstasy.

Mighty Michigan is down. The champions of four years have been outclassed and humiliated.

There arose in Ohio Stadium today a new national power in football, a colossus of the gridiron that may well follow on the glorious trail of Michigan, Southern Cal, Notre Dame and Minnesota.

Crash! That's Dick Heekin plunging through the shattered left side of the Michigan line for Ohio's touchdown only five minutes into the game.

That was for the team of 1902 that went up to Ann Arbor hopefully and was humiliated, 86-0.

Smack! That's Buzz Wetzel ramming through for the second touchdown, again through the Michigan line that once was so impregnable. That was for the team of 1926 that lost that heartbreaker here in this stadium before 90,000, 17-16.

Bang! That's Frank

Frank Antenucci's diving fumble recovery in the fourth quarter resulted in the Buckeyes' third touchdown.

Antenucci diving on a fumble for the third touchdown, starting a last-quarter avalanche.

There's the boom-boom-boom of Regis Monahan's big right toe, riding over those extra points. There's Frank Frisch, one of the goats of last year's crushing defeat at Ann Arbor, winging a tremendous pass to Merle Wendt for another touchdown.

There's that rabbit, Tippy Dye, hurling another pass to Frank Cumiskey for another TD.

The end of the rainbow — the dawn of a new era — for Michigan is down.

Nothing could detract from the satisfaction of this sweeping triumph — the largest, by 20 points, that Ohio has inflicted upon Michigan since 1897.

Michigan, beaten five times before this game, wasn't expected to do much, and it didn't.

If you want to know the extent of the shellacking, you can read it in these figures: OSU earned 24 first downs to Michigan's three (one by a penalty); OSU gained 319 yards rushing to Michigan's 6; OSU gained 141 yards passing to Michigan's 34.

"I feel as low as anyone could feel," said Michigan coach Harry Kipke. "Breaks — the good team always takes advantage of them. And Ohio was good."

And OSU coach Francis Schmidt, that middle-aged Nebraskan who tonight is the toast of Columbus, admitted reservedly that, "It was a wonderful game."

Wonderful? He doesn't know the half of it. But the jinx is dead and buried, and there are no goal posts out in the dark Ohio Stadium.

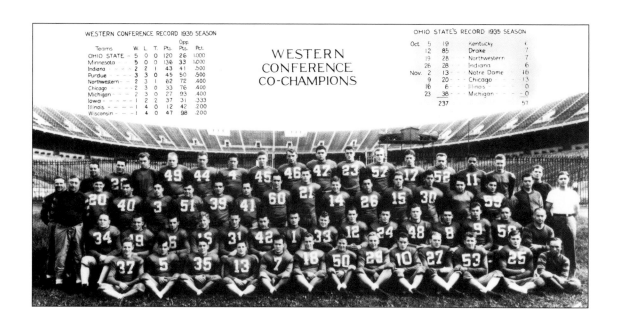

WESTERN CONFERENCE RECORD 1935 SEASON						
Teams	W.	L.	T.	Pts.	Opp Pts.	Pct.
OHIO STATE	5	0	0	120	26	1.000
Minnesota	5	0	0	136	33	1.000
Indiana	2	2	1	43	41	.500
Purdue	3	3	0	45	50	.500
Northwestern	2	3	1	62	72	.400
Chicago	2	3	0	33	76	.400
Michigan	2	3	0	27	93	.400
Iowa	1	2	2	37	31	.333
Illinois	1	4	0	12	42	.200
Wisconsin	1	4	0	47	98	.200

WESTERN CONFERENCE CO-CHAMPIONS

OHIO STATE'S RECORD 1935 SEASON			
Oct. 5	19	Kentucky	6
12	85	Drake	7
19	28	Northwestern	7
26	28	Indiana	6
Nov. 2	13	Notre Dame	18
9	20	Chicago	13
16	6	Illinois	0
23	38	Michigan	0
	237		57

NOTRE DAME SHOCKS OSU IN LAST MINUTE

Columbus, Nov. 2, 1935

Notre Dame	0	0	0	18	— 18
Ohio State	7	6	0	0	— 13

A great Notre Dame team – a team Knute Rockne would have loved, a team that could rise to magnificent, incredible heights of courage – shattered the glittering aspirations of Ohio State.

Wayne Millner caught a 19-yard touchdown pass from Bill Shakespeare in the final minute, giving the Irish an 18-13 victory.

Never, never, in all the miracles it has wrought, has Notre Dame ever done anything more tremendous than this – three touchdowns in the last quarter, against supposedly the strongest team in the country.

The Irish trailed 13-0 at the half. But a new Notre Dame came out for the second half. Coach Elmer Layden – Layden of the four Horsemen, who knew what Rock used to do between halves – had another team. He tossed aside his regulars, sat them down good and proper. He sent in an entirely new line.

Andy Pilney set up the first Irish TD with a 27-yard run to the Ohio State 13 as the third quarter ended.

A pass from Pilney to Frank Gaul took the ball to the 1, and fullback Steve Miller carried in from there.

After an Ohio State punt, the Irish got a first down on the Buckeye 8 on a pass interference call against Joe Zwers, but failed to score.

With only two minutes to go in the game, Pilney connected with Wally Fromhart for a 37-yard completion to the Ohio State 38.

Another forward pass, Mike Layden to Pilney. Pilney fumbled, but then Laurence Danbom from Calumet, Mich., (the hometown of George Gipp) gathered in the ball and was wrestled down on Ohio State's 29.

Francis A. Schmidt coached the Buckeyes from 1934 to 1940 and posted a 39-16-1 record.

The Ohio pass defense was collapsing. Pilney fired another pass, this one over center, to Fromhart and Notre Dame was on the 15 with a first down. From there it took only one play to score. Pilney threw to the left, and Layden raced to receive. The grand little halfback snagged the ball and went over the line. Touchdown, Notre Dame. The score is 13-12.

Notre Dame huddled. A point to tie and a minute and a half to go.

Fromhart was selected to kick and everything went wrong. The pass from center was too high and Pilney hardly had time to set up the ball. The kick bounced into the line of scrimmage, keeping the score 13-12.

Following the kick-off, OSU halfback Dick Beltz tried to plow off the Notre Dame left tackle. He fumbled and the ball bounced close to the sideline – almost out. Notre Dame's Henry Pojam was there just soon enough. He dived on the ball on the Irish 49.

On the next play, Pilney rushed back to pass. He was surrounded, so he whirled around, tucked the ball under his arm and went racing wildly 32 yards to Ohio State's 19.

But Pilney was hurt on the play and was carried out. Shakespeare took his place at left halfback.

There was time for two plays. Shakespeare darted out to the right and uncoiled a pass. Near the goal line, Beltz almost intercepted, but the

HERE

REAM LATERALED TO NARDI HERE

NARDI, C

In subsequent years, the lateral became a part of the OSU game plan (showcased here in a 1937 OSU contest), thanks to Frank Antenucci and Frank Boucher's heroics in the '35 Notre Dame game.

ball bounced from his chest.

One more chance.

Again, Shakespeare got the ball. Millner, more than 6 feet tall, ran for the end zone. Shakespeare threw and the ball soared toward Millner. A great roar filled the stadium ... a roar of awe, of disbelief. Millner spun around

and pulled the ball out of the air. A perfect pass, a perfect play. How Rockne would have loved it.

The 81,000 are standing. It can't be done, but they have seen it done. They have seen a Notre Dame miracle.

"Well, it was a great game. That's all I can say," Elmer Layden said.

Ohio State played well in the first half.

The first touchdown came like a thunderclap in the first five minutes. Stragglers of the 80,000

McDONALD PASSES TO REAM

were not yet in their seats, and Notre Dame, after an exchange of punts, seemed goalward bound.

Then it happened — a play that was attributable to the imagination of Coach Francis Schmidt.

But it was not without warning. This play had been prophesied by Schmidt in an article in the Saturday Evening Post early in the fall — a lateral after an interception.

In the first quarter, the Ohio State rush forced Layden into a poor pass near midfield. Frank Antenucci intercepted, and he lateraled to Frank Boucher. Boucher began galloping down the right side of the field.

As he reached the 20-yard line, Boucher was beyond pursuit. On he went over the line, while the great throng of Ohio supporters jumped from their seats. Beltz's extra point made it 7-0.

Joe Williams scored the Buckeyes' second touchdown on a 24-yard run, his ninth TD of the season.

OSU THRASHES MICHIGAN TO TIE FOR BIG TEN TITLE

Ann Arbor, Mich., Nov. 23, 1935					
Ohio State	13	6	6	13	– 38
Michigan	0	0	0	0	– 0

O hio State, arising in might and wrath to its full worth, annihilated Michigan, 38-0, and tied for the Big Ten Title.

Scoring six touchdowns, piling insult about injury, pounding for 60 minutes, Ohio State rolled up the score and shouted defiance at Minnesota.

Only by two points, matters of kicks after touchdowns, did Ohio fail to equal the total rolled up by Minnesota on the hapless Wolverines last week.

Two OSU touchdowns, one on a 50-yard run by Frank Boucher and another on a forward pass, Tippy Dye to

Sam Busich, were negated by penalties.

On this same field in Michigan Stadium, two years before, these same Ohio seniors, then sophomores, had taken a 13-0 defeat that Michigan has been crowing about ever since.

Tonight, in a somewhat plaintive whisper, they're still murmuring in Ann Arbor: "Anyhow, they're not as good as Minnesota."

To which any good Ohioan, in absolute sincerity, can answer: "Nuts."

They were plenty good enough, anyhow. They gave Michigan the worst licking it has ever taken from an OSU team, beating by four points the 34-0 score at Columbus last year. They gained 295 yards by passing, and made 20 first downs to Michigan's four.

And for the first time since 1920, since the day Pete Stinchcomb played his last game, the name of Ohio State is written with a

William Dye, who a week earlier scored the winner against Illinois, scored two touchdowns, including a 73-yard punt return.

percentage of 1.000 in the final Big Ten standings.

At the finish, OSU's rooters poured out of the stands and attacked the goal posts. Michigan students rallied around, and the fighting was beautiful to watch. The boys from Columbus finally did work a surprise attack, and rushed to the other end and felled the other set of goal posts, which were duly carted away.

Dick Heekin, one of the great power runners of all time, was impressive in this, his final game. When Heekin bullied into tacklers, they went over backwards. When he ripped at the line, he was a maniac.

Heekin scored two of the touchdowns, including the first one after about 10 minutes of play. Stunned in the third quarter, when he collided head-on with Bill Renner in trying to get a forward pass, Heekin had to leave the game. He came back in the final quarter, wilder than ever, and led another charge that ended in his second touchdown.

Then there was Stan Pincura, another senior who should be an All-American quarterback. Twice in the frantic last quarter, Pincura, back to pass on fourth down, took the ball himself, and bad shoulder and all, rammed his way for first downs.

William Dye, the 142-pound Pomeroy midget, made one touchdown, the second of the day, on a 73-yard run of a punt — a dash that for brilliance was even better than his 50-yard winning scamper against Illinois last week.

Nick Wasylik, the third of OSU's quarterbacks, made one of the scores from 24 yards out on a shovel pass, followed by two laterals. Wasylik popped the ball forward to end Sam Busich, who lateraled to fullback Jim McDonald. As McDonald was about to be tackled, he lateraled to Wasylik, who had come up from the rear.

A crowd of 65,000 spectators, three-fourths of them dumfounded Michigan supporters, saw the abject reduction of the maize and blue forces.

Wasylik, with some splendid broken field running, went 20 yards and over the line.

Frank Boucher of Kent, another senior, and John Bettridge of Toledo, a junior, were the other delighted backs who put the ball over hated Michigan's goal line.

Center Gomer Jones played two seasons for the Buckeyes and was an All-American in 1935.

BUCKEYES, LED BY DYE, VANQUISH MICHIGAN

Directing his team with brilliance that was a fitting climax to a glorious college gridiron career, Tippy Dye led Ohio State to its third straight victory over Michigan, 21-0.

The Pomeroy bantamweight – a 145-pounder, dripping wet – passed to Red Cumiskey for one touchdown. He whirled a shovel pass to set Johnny Rabb off on a 31-yard dash for another touchdown. He ran 55 yards, returning a punt, to within 6 yards of the Michigan goal, for what should have been another touchdown.

A crowd of 56,202, attesting once more to the popularity of the 39-year old OSU-Michigan series,

saw Coach Francis Schmidt's team equal one feat of the Chic Harley era. Until today, OSU had had only one three-year victory streak over the Wolverines – back in 1919, 1920 and 1921.

The crowd that braved increasing cold and swirling snow flurries in the last quarter brought Ohio's total attendance for the season to 391,375, a season's record by 37,000. The best previous mark for eight games was 354,941 in the boom days of 1929.

The final TD, in the fourth quarter, was made

by Nick Wasylik, a 151-pound substitute for Dye, on a run of 7 yards around Michigan's left end.

Ohio missed all its extra points. The three points that made it 21 came from a place kick from 12 yards out, booted for a field goal by Bill Booth, the East Liverpool sophomore.

Dye threw nine passes and completed six, one for a touchdown. That was in the second quarter, in which Dye connected on four of five passes in a sensational 76-yard march, finally flinging a 20-yarder to Cumiskey for the score.

Through the first half, which ended 6-0 for the Buckeyes, the game had been a fight — a real, old-fashioned Michigan-OSU donnybrook.

But the third quarter established OSU's superiority. There was an exchange of punts, punctuated by a nice 12-yard but fruitless gallop by Cedric Sweet. Then, from its 31, OSU went 69 yards in seven plays for the touchdown.

Rabb and Howard Wedebrook hammered out 7 yards on two plays. Rabb made a first down by inches on Ohio's 41.

Again Rabb splintered the Michigan defense for

Tackle Charles Hamrick was one of three OSU All-Americans on the 1936 team. The other two were guard Inwood Smith and end Merle Wendt.

nine yards, and then made another first down, on the Michigan 46.

Dye passed to Wedebrook for 14 yards and a first down on the 31.

Then, Dye feinted to his left, as if for an end run, and whisked a shovel pass to Rabb. The Akron sophomore departed through center, did an "S" curve through the Wolverine secondary and rambled down the right side of the field over the line.

Merle Wendt's extra-point kick was blocked but Ohio was well in command, 12-0.

A couple of minutes later, the razzle-dazzling continued with a shovel-lateral, Dye to Cumiskey to Rabb, good for 29 yards, to Michigan's 27. Another shovel, Rabb to Jumpin' Joe Williams, took the ball to the 12, but there the fighting Wolverines held for three downs. Booth missed a placement for field goal from the 15.

But Dye was not to be denied. Michigan was held at its 20 after the touchback and punted out.

Dye took the ball on OSU's 39 and was off to the races before finally being hauled down at the 6. Booth's 12-yard field goal made it 15-0.

BUCKEYES ROMP OVER MICHIGAN, 21-0

T he Ohio State battle cry shrills once more from the depths of the great Michigan Stadium.

Ohio State's big rough-housing line, in its farewell appearance of a great season, today once more manhandled Michigan, 21-0.

For the fourth straight year, by a score that hardly measures the scarlet superiority, OSU completely routed and overwhelmed its oldest and most bitter Big Ten rival. OSU became the second team in history to defeat Michigan four times in succession. Minnesota completed the trick earlier in the season.

Ann Arbor, Mich., Nov. 21, 1937					
Ohio State	0	7	7	7	– 21
Michigan	0	0	0	0	– 0

A crowd of 60,000 frozen fans saw the 34th game of the historic series that began in 1897. The battle was waged in bitter cold. There was snowfall throughout the second half, reaching blizzard proportions as the game ended.

OSU, with five victories and one defeat (the upset by Indiana) ended second in the Big Ten, as Minnesota wound up undefeated, the champion.

A fighting Michigan eleven, in the game only briefly during the first half, yielded before the supercharged assaults of OSU's grand seniors.

Jim Miller of Shelby, a third stringer, piled over the Michigan line for two touchdowns.

His first score, in the last second of the first half, came on a blast through Michigan's left tackle, from the 2-yard line. His second touchdown came on a superb pass play, good for 44 yards, from Nick Wasylik, in which Miller raced 17 yards through fluffy snowfall. Not a Michigan man was near him.

The other touchdown was scored by Nick Nardi, the Collinwood right halfback. On a pass from Wasylik, from 11 yards out, the crashing Nardi carried a Michigan tackler 3 yards with him and over the line.

Jim McDonald, the fullback-quarterback and co-captain, ending a career that should land him on the All-America team, kicked one extra point. OSU's other two points, in the second quarter, were on a safety in which Charley Ream, senior end, tackled Norm Purucker, Michigan halfback, behind the goal line.

Purucker, a 170-pound junior from Poland, Ohio, played a tremendous, heroic game for the lost cause of Michigan. His great punting time and again hurled back the charging OSU giants. A dozen times, after his kick, he tore down the field and made the tackle of the OSU receiver.

Never has an OSU team, which had reason to be overconfident, looked in better mental condition. The great charging line, featuring such stalwarts as Gus Zarnas, Carl Kaplanoff and Ralph Wolf, spared Michigan not at all. The Buckeyes were there to win, and by the biggest possible score.

The game ended with the Ohio subs, after a slashing march down the field, half a yard from the maize and blue goal again. One second more might have meant another touchdown.

OSU, though making only seven first downs, gained 194 yards by rushing and 101 by passing.

In four years under Francis Schmidt, OSU has scored 114 points on Michigan. The Buckeye goal line, under the Schmidt regime, never has been touched by Michigan. The Wolverines haven't made a point on Ohio State since that bitter October day in Michigan Stadium back in 1933, when Michigan conquered one of the biggest OSU teams, 13-0.

Michigan's net gain against OSU's line, from rushing, was exactly 8 yards. In passing, the Wolverines added 37 yards.

Michigan put up a valiant fight, in defense of the wavering coaching regime of Harry Kipke. But the Wolverines could not cope with OSU's power.

Quarterback Jim McDonald earned All-American honors in 1937, but more importantly, he helped the Buckeyes shut out the Wolverines in Ann Arbor.

OSU GIVES GOPHERS BOOT

Ohio State bombarded Minnesota with a bewildering assortment of forward and lateral passes to triumph, 23-20, and become the first Big Ten team to whip the Gophers on their home sod since 1932.

Three times the scarlet-jerseyed Buckeyes split Minnesota's pass defenses wide open and poured over touchdowns, but it was Charley Maag's second-quarter field goal from the 20-

Minneapolis, Oct. 21, 1939						
Ohio State	0	16	7	0	–	23
Minnesota	7	7	0	6	–	20

yard line that kept Ohio State among the nation's major undefeated, untied teams.

Playing straight football, Minnesota sent its homecoming crowd of 50,000 into a frenzy by scoring late in the first quarter after an Ohio State fumble had given the Gophers possession

JOHNSON, S.—MINN.

STRAUSBAUGH—O.

Minnesota had trouble stopping Jim Strausbaugh and OSU (top photo). Quarterback Don Scott (9), Coach Francis Schmidt (center) and Earl Langhurst (8) helped lead the Buckeyes to a Big Ten championship in 1939.

on the Buckeyes' 13-yard line.

Ohio State didn't wait long. In the second period, quarterback Don Scott rifled two touchdown passes and Maag drove his angled kick squarely through the uprights for a total of 16 points while Minnesota was scoring seven. Scott again tossed a touchdown pass in the third quarter and the

Gophers barely missed tying the score in the final minutes of play when a 28-yard placekick struck the crossbar and fell back into the end zone.

After the Bucks rolled their lead up to 23-14 midway through the third quarter, the game turned into one of the roughest Big Ten clashes in years. Twice little George Franck came off the ground swinging after hard tackles, once sending the entire Ohio State squad and Coach Francis Schmidt off the bench to intervene. No penalties were called, much to the surprise of both coaches and fans.

Minnesota scored in four plays after John Marlucci recovered Jim Strausbaugh's first-quarter fumble on Ohio State's 13. Franck made a first down on the 2, and on the third play of the series, Marty Christiansen scored.

The Bucks then opened a 76-yard touchdown drive, climaxing the march in the second quarter with Scott's forward pass to Esco Sarkkinen for a score from 32 yards out.

But the Bucks came bounding back after a short punt and scored in two plays from the Minnesota 45.

Scott's third and last touchdown pass occurred in the third quarter after the Buckeyes took the ball on Minnesota's 45, where Strausbaugh recovered an attempted lateral by Christiansen.

Quarterback Don Scott threw three touchdown passes, including two in the second quarter, to lead the Buckeyes past the Gophers.

Ohio State drove to the 34 and from there, Scott passed to Frank Clare in the end zone. Scott kicked the extra point.

The fourth quarter was all Minnesota. The Gophers scored on the first play, Van Every passing to Bruce Smith.

The superiority of Ohio State's deadly passing game is shown in the statistics, which gave them 166 yards and three touchdowns to Minnesota's 48 yards and one TD. The Gophers excelled at rushing, getting 238 to the Buckeyes' 128. Ohio State completed 10 of 13 passes and Minnesota connected with only 2 of 7. Minnesota got 11 first downs to Ohio's 10.

Both coaches criticized the officiating of the game, but the loudest complaints came from Bernie Bierman, who declared, "laxity in officiating was inexcusable," and claimed wrong decisions always gave Ohio State the advantage, never Minnesota.

Each of the coaches had a private tale of woe to tell. Schmidt's concerned Earl Langhurst's 80-yard touchdown run in the third quarter that was called back when Ohio State was penalized five yards for backfield in motion.

"It takes all the enjoyment out of the game," Schmidt moaned.

WESTERN CONFERENCE AND NATIONAL CHAMPIONS - 1942

BUCKEYES RIDE OVER INDIANA'S HILLENBRAND

Columbus, Oct. 3, 1942					
Indiana	0	7	14	0 –	21
Ohio State	6	7	6	13 –	32

O hio State caught the full fury of Indiana's Billy Hillenbrand, but gave it back with plenty to spare and emerged triumphant in an eye-popping scoring duel that opened the Big Ten season, 32-21.

With fullback Gene Fekete and right halfback Leslie Horvath matching the dazzling runs of Hillenbrand and another Hoosier who looks just as good – sophomore Bob Cowan – the plucky Buckeyes came back from behind to score twice in the

last quarter and win decisively.

A crowd of 48,227 saw a gridiron battle that was a spectator's game every minute. It resembled OSU's "track meet" victory over Wisconsin last season.

OSU got the first two touchdowns, marching 57 yards for the first in less than seven minutes and tallying again early in the second quarter after a pass interference penalty had put the ball on the

BUCKEYES VS. INDIANA, 1942

After a pass interference call put the ball on the Indiana 1-yard line, Paul Sarringhaus (88) scored to give Ohio State a 13-0 lead early in the second quarter.

tackle and sped 45 yards for the third OSU touchdown, and the Buckeyes were ahead again, 19-14.

Then it was Indiana's turn once more. Using a nice mixture of passes and rushes, the Hoosiers put on their only long march of the day, going 65 yards with quarterback Lou Saban scoring on a 7-yard pass from Hillenbrand.

The score then stood 21-19, Indiana having converted all its extra points. The Buckeyes missed two out of three.

Indiana faded in the final quarter.

Hoosier 1-yard line. Fekete scored the first touchdown and Paul Sarringhaus the second.

At this point it looked like a rout, but in the seventh minute of the second quarter Hillenbrand burst through the line and darted 54 yards for a touchdown. It was 13-7 for OSU at the half.

The game was just warming up. On the fourth play of the second half, Cowan, the sensational sophomore, swept around OSU's right end and galloped 46 yards for a touchdown to put the Hoosiers ahead.

Just five plays after that, Fekete jammed through

Fekete scored his third touchdown, finishing a 35-yard OSU advance, in the fourth minute of the final quarter. He made the point after, and it was 26-21.

To the 48,000 fans it was anything but a sure thing. Les Horvath, the 180-pound senior from Cleveland, finally clinched it with two beautiful runs after George Lynn had intercepted a Hoosier pass on the Ohio State 29. Horvath's first dash was 13 yards and his second 15 yards to the Indiana 1. Lynn rammed through center to make the final score 32-21.

Twice in the last 10 minutes Tommy Massilon intercepted Indiana passes to throttle every Hoosier effort to get going once more.

Ohio State gained 341 yards rushing to Indiana's 179, and 108 yards passing to Indiana's 78. Ohio State completed 5 of 15 passes and Indiana 5 of 16.

Brown's Teachings and Goals Are Still in Place Today at OSU

He didn't stay long, not even as long as most players.

Time, though, isn't the measure by which Paul Brown's three-year influence on the Ohio State football program can be judged. Not if it's to be judged accurately.

The problem with time is it's hemmed in by numbers and the limiting notions that form in people's minds as they process what can be accomplished within those numbers.

An hour isn't so much 60 minutes as it is the start-to-finish estimate of a few errands in the neighborhood.

A month isn't so much 30 days as it is the break between the next batch of bills to be mailed out.

And three football seasons? Why, that just isn't long enough for a coach to achieve much more than minimal impact, unless it's negative impact.

For some men, maybe even most men, that might be true.

But Paul Brown wasn't most men, and he certainly wasn't most football coaches.

Not on the high school level at Massillon Washington, where his teams went 80-8-2 over his nine-year career and 58-1-1 from 1935-40.

Not on the professional level with the Cleveland Browns, where he went 167-53-9 and won seven championships in 17 seasons.

Not with the Cincinnati Bengals, which he took from an expansion team to the NFL playoffs in three seasons.

And certainly not on the collegiate level at Ohio State.

Though his time on the sidelines in Columbus lasted only from 1941-43, Brown's achievements with the Buckeyes so shaped the expectations for the program that the very goals he established are still in place today.

The absolute intolerance for losing, especially to Michigan, flourished because of the success Brown's teams enjoyed in fashioning a 15-2-1 record his first two years before World War II intruded and left OSU a defenseless 3-6 his final year.

Team MVP Jack Graf (left) said Coach Paul Brown was "very organized and very disciplined." Thomas Kinkade is on the right.

The insatiable thirst for a national championship that consumes OSU loyalists to this day took root with the school's first title won — in Brown's second season.

So did the notion that victory is a Buckeye birthright, for in the eight years after Brown departed, OSU acquired an unflattering image as "the graveyard of coaches" while searching for someone ... anyone ... to duplicate what Brown had done.

Ohio State finally found its man in Woody Hayes, another eventual coaching legend, and it is only the enormity of what Hayes achieved in 28 seasons that pushed Brown's success at OSU into the background.

Brown never minded that, and he never wavered when asked which of his many accomplishments in the sport gave him his greatest pleasure.

Upon his acceptance of the National Football Foundation's prestigious gold medal award in 1989, Brown told a crowded ballroom at New York's Waldorf Astoria: "The most exciting of all the jobs I had was at Ohio State."

It must be true, then. First loves really do last the longest and forgive the most.

That much, we know, because Brown's first expo-sure to Ohio State wasn't the stuff of dreams.

It was the stuff of nightmares.

Having been an accomplished quarterback at Massillon himself, Brown arrived on the OSU campus in the fall of 1926 eager to begin duplicating the collegiate football success his predecessor in high school, Harry Stuhldreher, was enjoying as one of the famed Four Horsemen at Notre Dame.

It takes a uniform to gain fame in football, however, and Ohio State wasn't inclined to waste one on a spindly, 17-year-old.

Brown, therefore, was rebuffed in his attempts to join the OSU freshman team because he was judged too small.

That precipitated a transfer to Miami University, where Brown starred at quarterback and developed the thirst for coaching that took him back to his high school alma mater just three years after his college graduation.

The Tigers had won only one game the previous year, during which their 3,000-seat stadium sat virtually empty and the school's $37,000 athletic budget bled red ink.

By the time Brown left nine years later, the stadium had been expanded to 21,000 and the team

In his first two seasons at OSU, Paul Brown was 15-2-1 and had an intolerance for losing, especially to Michigan.

drew 182,000 fans his final year, generating more than $100,000 in revenue and making Ohio State Athletic Director Lynn W. St. John's choice of a new football coach an obvious selection.

"Even though I had considered their refusal to give me a uniform the cruelest injustice, my love for the place had never diminished," Brown wrote in his 1991 autobiography, *PB: The Paul Brown Story*. "In the evenings (while attending summer school), I'd often go to the stadium, walk about the playing surface and then sit on the Ohio State bench. I'd close my eyes and imagine myself coaching the Buckeyes and visualize what it might be like with the stadium

When not roaming the sidelines, Paul Brown enjoyed spending time with his wife and two sons, Michael (left) and Robin.

jammed and the game unfolding before me."

Those daydreams gave way to reality when Brown was named head coach at a salary of $6,500, becoming at age 33 the youngest head coach in the history of the Big Ten and the first high school coach ever hired to lead the Ohio State program.

Brown, though, brought the assurance of a much more experienced coach with him to Columbus.

"Right from the start, the difference between

Paul Brown and Francis Schmidt was very evident," said Jack Graf, a backup quarterback under Schmidt in 1940 who was switched to fullback by Brown and became Big Ten MVP in 1941. "Paul Brown was very organized and very disciplined. He knew what he wanted and he was willing to adjust his offense to the ability of his players."

Brown's Buckeyes were so well-schooled it delivered them from disaster in his debut against Missouri.

Ironically, St. John's second choice as head coach after Brown was Missouri's Don Faurot.

That gave Faurot plenty of incentive to try to spoil the Buckeyes' 1941 season opener, and he mustered all his ingenuity to invent the Split T formation as a surprise.

Missouri used that offense to move the football at will, but Brown's defensive fundamentals held steady and delivered a 12-7 victory the rookie head coach almost didn't get to witness.

Upon entering the stadium that day, Brown had lingered to speak with some friends from Massillon and then came across probably the only man in Columbus who didn't know what the new Ohio State coach looked like.

"You can't come in here, sir, without a ticket," the guard at the gate said to Brown.

"I don't have a ticket, I'm Paul Brown," Brown said.

"Is that right? Well, I'm President Roosevelt," the guard responded, "and you still can't come in."

By the following week, everyone across the United States knew Brown, for his Buckeyes went west and shocked heavily-favored Southern California, 33-0.

OSU's only loss that season came two weeks lat-

Paul Brown (center) was all smiles after Paul Sarringhaus (left) scored twice and Gene Fekete (right) scored once in a 20-6 win at Northwestern.

er to Northwestern, 14-7, but even in defeat Brown gained something. He took note that day of a sophomore single-wing tailback and his unique abilities to both run and pass.

Five years later, Otto Graham became the first player Brown signed for his new team in the All-America Football Conference.

Graham would lead the Browns to the championship game of either that league or the NFL every year of the decade he played professionally, winning seven titles in all.

At times in Cleveland, the Browns featured an Ohio State-laden line of Bill Willis and Lou Groza at tackle, Lin Houston and Bob Gaudio at guard, and Dante Lavelli at end.

Willis, Houston and Lavelli were mainstays up front on OSU's once-beaten, 1942 national champions, a team whose preseason prospects were modest because of the graduation of Graf and the entire offensive backfield.

"We didn't know what to expect that year and no one knew what to expect of us," said Paul Sarringhaus, who joined eventual Heisman Trophy winner Les Horvath in taking over at the two single-wing tailback spots that season. "We set our sights on winning the Big Ten championship, never thinking about anything else."

Certainly not about contaminated drinking water, but that's about all that stopped the Buckeyes that season.

With the war effort commandeering all the best of the country's rail-

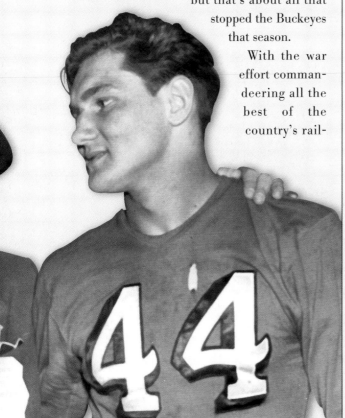

road equipment, it was a long-mothballed rail car that OSU boarded for a trip to Wisconsin in mid-season.

Trouble was, old railroad cars often held old rusty water in their storage tanks, and the top-ranked Buckeyes came down with a serious case of dysentery en route to Madison.

The resultant 17-7 defeat looked like it might end OSU's championship dream, but the Badgers lost the following week to Iowa and the Buckeyes were back in the title chase.

Sarringhaus made sure they didn't stumble again, throwing for two touchdowns and catching another scoring pass from Horvath in the 21-7 victory over Michigan that gave Ohio State the conference title.

All that remained was a late add-on to the schedule against Iowa Pre-Flight, a military training academy stocked with former collegiate All-Americans and professionals, coached by Minnesota's legendary Bernie Bierman, who had won six Big Ten championships over the previous eight seasons.

Third-ranked OSU jumped to a 27-6 halftime lead and coasted to a 41-12 victory on the same day No. 1 Georgia fell to Georgia Tech and No. 2 Boston College lost to lowly Holy Cross.

That left Ohio State an overwhelming choice as the national champions, but the glow of a season in which Brown's team set a school scoring record of 337 points that stood for another 27 years soon faded.

The war effort intruded and claimed most of Brown's senior-laden roster by 1943, leaving him to battle with what would become known as "the baby Buckeyes."

"My first two years at Ohio State were the happiest, most exciting and most rewarding period of my life, better in some respect than the years in Cleveland, because coaching the Buckeyes had been my ultimate dream," Brown wrote before his death in 1991.

FOURTH-QUARTER RALLY
FELLS MICHIGAN

A t long last, the great dream came true. After nearly a quarter century of painful disappointments, Ohio State went all the way. Led by that terrific one-man Parma typhoon, Lee Horvath, the greatest college halfback in the country, the brilliant Buckeyes of 1944 completed their first perfect record in 24 years by defeating a rough and courageous Michigan team, 18-14.

Behind at the end of the first quarter, 7-6, and trailing, 14-12, with less than nine minutes remaining in the final quarter, the scrapping Buckeyes

Columbus, Nov. 25, 1944						
Michigan	0	7	0	7	–	14
Ohio State	6	0	6	6	–	18

came raging from behind to deliver the winning touchdown with 3:16 left.

And as Horvath, diving headlong, barreled over for the winning score, with a mob of 71,958 fans hysterical with excitement, Ohio State completed its first perfect regular season – and undefeated and untied – since 1920.

With this tremendous achievement accomplished by an all-civilian team, without aid of Navy or Army trainees, went the undisputed Big Ten championship — six straight victories.

Horvath carried the ball 33 times, gained 104 yards and scored both of OSU's touchdowns in the second half.

And not lost in the plaudits is Carroll Widdoes, the Ohio State coach, who in his first season as the head coach of a college team (as a sub until Paul Brown returns from his Navy service) accomplished what no other OSU coach has been able to do since the day of Pete Stinchcomb and Hoge Workman.

The second time they got hold of the ball, in the first quarter, the Buckeyes unleashed their driving power and marched 56 yards to a touchdown, with fullback Ollie Cline hitting through guard for the score. Jack Dugger's kick for point was blocked by Harold Watts, the Michigan center.

Ohio continued to hold the upper hand until late in the second quarter, when an intercepted pass, by Ralph Chubb, paved the way for a Michigan touchdown scored by Bill Culligan with only 22 seconds of the half left. Quarterback Joe Ponsetto's kick for point sent the Wolverines ahead, 7 to 6.

Michigan came bursting out for the second half, carried the ball 26 yards to OSU's 35 in four plays, and then fumbled. Twice in the first few minutes of the third quarter, Gordon Appleby, the OSU center, playing his last game, recovered Michigan fumbles.

After the second of these, the Buckeyes went 23 yards to take the lead, Horvath plunging for the last

yard. Tom Keane tried the extra point this time, and missed, and it was 12-7 for OSU.

But as the last quarter opened, it was the Wolverines' turn. They were underway with a masterful, smashing rush that went 83 yards, during which they completed the only forward pass of the game, Culligan to Ponsetto, for 28 yards. Culligan ripped off tackle for the score with 8:29 left, and Ponsetto's placement for point made it 14-12.

Michigan, on the kickoff, tried an onside kick. The ball sliced left and went out of bounds on OSU's 48. It was a strategy that backfired.

From the 48, the Buckeyes marched downfield. Horvath, once more, dove high over right guard and came down with the ball over the goal line.

Lee Horvath, the Parma typhoon, carried the Buckeyes to victory over the Wolverines with two second-half touchdowns.

HAGUE GIVES OSU ROSEY FINISH TO '49 SEASON

Pasadena, Calif., Jan. 2, 1950						
Ohio State	0	0	14	3	–	17
California	0	7	7	0	–	14

A favorite son of Greater Cleveland delivered the grandest victory in the history of Ohio State football for OSU.

Plucky Jimmy Hague, the cheerful, rugged 200-pound senior end from Rocky River, won the Rose Bowl game.

With 1:55 to go, the mighty 21-year old warrior – his No. 80 blazing in the floodlights – kicked a field goal from the 17-yard line that conquered the Golden Bears of California, 17-14.

The terrific roar of fans in the Rose Bowl bounced off the backdrop of the Sierra Madres and rolled down the Arroyo Seco toward Los Angeles.

Never a day like this for Ohio State. Never a day like this for Jimmy Hague, or for his father, mother, aunt and uncle, cheering with the mob, or for young Tommy Hague, his kid

OSU fullback Fred Morrison (33) picks up 15 yards before California's Paul Baldwin (34) can bring him down.

brother, sitting back there in Cleveland, listening to the radio.

The broad-shouldered young man, with nerves of steel, and a kicking toe that ranks with the greatest in the game, maintained the Big Ten supremacy over the Pacific Coast.

It's the fourth straight year the Midwesterners have traveled west and lashed the Pacific gladiators on their home course in the super-glamour setting of Pasadena's famous arena.

It was 14-14 and there were three minutes to go as Bob Celeri, the brilliant California quarterback, became the victim of a crack-up that led to his team's defeat.

With the ball on the Bears' 16, Celeri tried to punt on fourth down. He fumbled the pass from center and tried to run. Chuck Gilbert, the big Buckeye defensive end, gave chase. Celeri, in desperation, on the lope, hesitated momentarily and then tried a kick anyhow. The ball bobbled out of bounds on the California 13.

Thirteen yards to go, and the game at stake — a victory that would bring Ohio revenge for that 18-0 defeat way back in 1921.

The raging Buckeyes fairly ripped into the dark blue-shirted California line. Jerry Krall hit tackle to the 10, and fullback Fred (Curly) Morrison, a great pile driver as always, went to the 9. Krall lashed tackle to just outside the 5.

It was fourth down with two yards to go. Two OSU players came running into the game. It cost OSU a 5-yard penalty for delay — but the order had come from Coach Wes Fesler. The command was to kick.

The ball was put back to just outside the California 10. Dick Widdoes got set to hold the ball.

One step by Hague and then — boom! Victory was floating high and straight over the crossbar. Hague previously had booted two extra points that held the battle even at 14. He hasn't missed a conversion since Oct. 8. He's the boy who has kicked OSU in all the way — from the 35-34 victory over Missouri to the 7-7 tie with Michigan, and the final, tremendous triumph here today.

As the mass of worshipful fans and players moved

Running back Fred (Curly) Morrison was named MVP in the 1950 Rose Bowl with 113 yards rushing on 25 attempts.

slowly off the field, Hague and Fesler were carried on Buckeye shoulders through the archway to the OSU dressing room.

It was perhaps — and sadly — also Fesler's last college game. The coach's resignation to enter business is expected shortly. He retires at the peak of the coaching profession as pilot of the Rose Bowl champions of 1950.

"Who has the best band?" yelled the OSU cheerleader, through his loudspeaker.

"Ohio State," was the murmured return.

"And who has the best team?" he continued.

This time it was a roar – "Ohio State!" The OSU fans who had traveled all the way across the continent to be here had waited a long time for this moment.

These Golden Bears, who had been beaten by Northwestern, 20-14, in another heartbreaker here last season, were very tough.

Jim Monachino, the one-time John Adams High freshman who migrated to Southern California, scored both Cal touchdowns. His first, in

Buckeyes Coach Wes Fesler presents actress Esther Williams with an autographed football during the team's visit to Hollywood.

the second quarter, was on a 7-yard dash around end.

The other, in the third quarter, was on a magnificent, 44-yard gallop around the right side of the OSU line, after the Buckeyes had taken a 14-7 lead.

The score was 7-0 at the half. OSU took over in the style typical of this Buckeye squad in the third quarter, scoring twice, with Morrison and Krall carrying over. It was a battle full of sensational plays, and a glittering finale of Pasadena's 61st Tournament of Roses in which an estimated 1,750,000 spectators watched the incredible parade in the morning.

OSU made 19 first downs to California's 12, and 221 yards rushing to the Bears' 133. California led in passing yardage, 106 to 34, thanks to one great play that rivaled the legendary 53-yard throw by Harold P. (Brick) Muller to Brodie Stephens back in 1921 in Cal's smashing victory over OSU.

This mighty pass that led to Monachino's first touchdown was hurled by Celeri to halfback Frank Brunk. The gain covered 55 yards, from the California 26 to Ohio's 19.

The game was played in cold, clammy weather, with even topcoats not enough to keep warm, the sky overcast and much like the gray days of November back home. Though the field was dry, the thin turf and loose base bothered Ohio runners in swift cutbacks, particularly Krall.

Floodlights were turned on for the last quarter.

Hague's kick won the game, but it was Morrison and Krall, the two workhorses of the OSU backfield all season, who carried through to the finish.

Morrison gained 113 yards on 25 attempts, Krall 80 yards in 28 tries. These are two real stars who were missed entirely in the All-American selections.

In a driving snowstorm and 10-degree temperatures, Michigan put the freeze on Ohio State's Rose Bowl plans.

BUCKEYES GO COLD AS U-M STORMS ON TO ROSE BOWL

I n the most amazing climax in Big Ten history, Michigan today conquered a raging blizzard and Ohio State, 9-3, to win the Western Conference title and the bid to the Rose Bowl at Pasadena, Jan. 1.

On a day when football never should have been attempted, the resourceful and stout-hearted Wolverines ended triumphant in a struggle through the driving snow in 10-degree temperature.

Michigan won on two blocked punts, one for a safety and the other for a touchdown. The only

Columbus, Nov. 25, 1950					
Michigan	2	7	0	0 –	9
Ohio State	3	0	0	0 –	3

offensive score of the bitter cold day was a 28-yard field goal — 38 from the goal posts — kicked with the wind through the uprights by Vic Janowicz of Ohio State in the first five minutes of the game.

It was the fourth straight year in which Michigan has won or tied for the Big Ten title — undisputed in 1947, 1948 and this year, and a tie with Ohio last season.

46

BUCKEYES VS. MICHIGAN, 1950

Master of this game, the man who turned the tide, was Charles (Chuck) Ortmann, the great Michigan left halfback.

Ortmann won the game with his beautiful placement of punts. He kicked OSU into a corner from which it could not fight its way out. A determined, hard-hitting Michigan line did the rest with two blocked punts.

The conditions were beyond description. They were infinitely worse than those for the famous zero game between the Cleveland Rams and the Washington Redskins for the National Football League title in 1945 in Cleveland Stadium.

The field lines were covered by snow, though the gridiron had been covered by tarpaulins, which were taken off — only with considerable effort by a 100-man crew — just before the game.

Ball carrying was impossible. Michigan gained 27 yards rushing and OSU 16. Michigan never made a first down and never completed a pass. Ohio managed to complete three passes in 18 attempts for 23 yards.

The attendance was announced as 50,503, though it didn't look as if there were more than 30,000 frozen fans huddled in the stadium. At any rate, more than 35,000 who had tickets did not appear.

Michigan won the conference title with a league record of four victories, one defeat, and one tie, edg-

With weather conditions more suitable for penguins, 35,000 fans with tickets decided to stay home by the fire.

ing Ohio State, with five wins and two defeats.

Thus a Michigan team beaten by Army, Michigan State and Illinois and tied by lowly Minnesota, goes to the Rose Bowl.

With Ohio leading on Janowicz's field goal, 3-0, Michigan got its first points late in the first period on a blocked punt that rolled across the end zone and out of bounds. This punt was blocked by one of the big Michigan tacklers, Al Wahl or Tom Johnson, or both.

The Michigan touchdown came with only 20 seconds left in the first half, when Tony Momsen, the big Michigan linebacker, blocked another of Janowicz's punts, chased the ball across the goal line, and fell on it. Harry Allis kicked the conversion.

47

CASSADY'S "HOPALONG" DOOMS WISCONSIN

Columbus, Oct. 23, 1954

Wisconsin	0	7	0	7 —	14
Ohio State	0	3	7	21 —	31

Howard (Hopalong) Cassady, a red-headed Irishman with the speed of a deer and the heart of a lion, touched off one of the most impressive scoring explosions in Ohio State history.

His nose scarred, his right hand bandaged, the 168-pound Cassady intercepted a pass and dashed 88 yards for a touchdown, sending the Buckeyes past Wisconsin, 31-14.

With Ohio State trailing, 7-3, and the third quarter nearly over, Cassady's dramatic and incredible dash did more than just turn impending defeat into victory.

His sensational touchdown sprint set off the dynamite in a previously staggering and stumbling OSU attack. It wrecked the poise of a confident Wisconsin team that had not been scored on in the second half this season.

The Badgers cracked and faded. The Buckeyes erupted as if touched off by an electric spark.

In seven minutes of the last quarter, the inspired Buckeyes shredded the Badger defense for three more touchdowns.

Quarterback Dave Leggett found a hole, avoided tacklers and crossed the goal line to give OSU a 24-7 fourth-quarter lead.

By actual count, the rampant OSU machine made four touchdowns in about nine minutes against a Wisconsin team that had gone into the game ranked No. 2 in the nation.

It was OSU's fifth straight victory, and its fourth in a row in the Big Ten. The Buckeyes now share the conference lead with surprising Michigan.

A packed house of 82,636, one of the largest in the history of Ohio Stadium, watched the Buckeyes' phenomenal display.

The defeat was Wisconsin's first after four straight wins, and might ruin the Badgers' hopes of a Rose Bowl bid.

No threatening defeat ever turned into triumph so quickly.

Early in the second quarter, OSU had taken a 3-0 lead when Thurlow (Tad) Weed, 148-pound place-kicking specialist, booted a field goal from the 29-yard line (39 yards from the posts).

At 13:10 of the second quarter, Wisconsin went ahead on a 35-yard touchdown pass, quarterback Jim Miller to halfback Pat Levenhagen.

Glen Wilson's conversion point put the Badgers in front, 7-3.

There the score hung through most of the hard-fought third quarter.

Another Wisconsin touchdown seemed certain as the Badgers, passing and running expertly, ground toward the goal.

Alan Ameche, Wisconsin's All-America fullback, had just slammed through 6 yards to the Ohio 20. It was second down, 4 to go.

Miller had been having exceptional luck with his passes. For the day, he completed 11 of 19. But the pass is a dangerous weapon.

With the ball on the 20, Miller aimed one over the middle. Cassady picked off the ball on the 12.

Before the Badgers could recover he was gone down the left side of the field.

Weed kicked the point and OSU led, 10-7, at 12:52.

That was good, but for what was coming, the roaring crowd was entirely unprepared.

Wisconsin rallied and had the ball on OSU's 34 as the quarter ended.

As the last quarter started, Pat Levenhagen, plowing at right tackle, fumbled as he was hit by Jerry Williams. Fullback Hubert Bobo dove on the ball on the OSU 30.

Jim Parker was an All-American guard in 1955 and 1956. He also was the team's MVP in '56.

Then, with an atomic burst, OSU went 70 yards in four plays. Cassady sped around right end for 40 yards.

Bob Watkins made eight yards around end, to the Badger 22. Quarterback Dave Leggett lobbed a short, soft pass to Watkins, who was uncovered on the Wisconsin 4. In one smash, Bobo was over, and Weed kicked again to make it 17-7, at 1:37 of the quarter.

The Badgers then went to pieces. Miller decided to pass his way back into the game, but Wisconsin was stopped on its 39.

It was fourth down there, with a punting set-up, as a sad error in strategy was attempted. Bob Gingrass, in the punter's position, received the ball and tried a flat pass to the right to sophomore Billy Lowe.

This backfired to complete Wisconsin's ruin. End Dean Dugger chased Lowe back for a 12-yard loss and it was OSU's ball on the Wisconsin 28.

Leggett, in one sprint in which he faked a pitchout beautifully, ran around the Badger right side all the way for another touchdown. Watkins kicked and OSU led, 24-7.

Still, it wasn't over. Lowe, on the 10, took the

kickoff and returned 20 yards, but his knee had touched the ground on the 10.

From that spot, Charlie Thomas, who subs for Ameche at fullback, tried an off-tackle play. He fumbled and tackle Don Swartz recovered on the Wisconsin 10.

Once more it took only one play. Jerry Harkrader of Middletown, the junior who relieves Cassady, darted the 10 yards in a brilliant cutback. Watkins kicked again, and it was 31-7.

Cassady is perhaps the greatest nemesis in the history of Badger football. Cassady's greatest running and pass catching led OSU to an upset triumph over Wisconsin, 23-14, here in 1952.

Last season at Madison, with OSU behind, 19-7, going into the last quarter, Cassady eventually won the game, 20-19, on a 60-yard touchdown pass play from Leggett.

Ameche, in his fourth and last try against OSU, has never scored on the Buckeyes. In 16 attempts

A packed house of 82,636 at Ohio Stadium watched the Buckeyes score 28 second-half points against the Badgers.

in this game, Ameche gained only 42 yards.

Cassady, who grew up in Columbus, played with a gash across his nose and his right hand encased in a rubber sponge bandage.

His nose was nearly broken and his hand had a four-stitch wound during the 20-14 victory over Iowa here last week.

Wisconsin did well on the statistics sheet, if not on the scoreboard. The Badgers gained 357 yards of offense to 241 for OSU. In first downs, Wisconsin had 19 and Ohio State 12.

Cassady gained 59 yards in seven rushing attempts. Watkins made 43 yards in 12 tries. Leggett completed 5 of 14 passes for 62 yards. Cassady, in addition to his game-breaking interception, also caught two passes for 23 yards.

The Buckeyes celebrate the victory over Michigan and a trip to Pasadena for the Rose Bowl against USC.

BUCKEYES TOP MICHIGAN

Ohio State's tremendous football machine goes to the Rose Bowl unbeaten, untied, winner of nine straight, undisputed champion of the Big Ten and maybe the No. 1 team of the nation.

In a spectacular exhibition of valor and perseverance, the mighty Buckeyes battled back to defeat Michigan, 21-7.

Columbus, Nov. 20, 1954					
Michigan	7	0	0	0	– 7
Ohio State	0	7	0	14	– 21

Battered to the ropes early in the game, the beleaguered Buckeyes tied the score after an interception, and then drove to decisive victory with two touchdowns in the last quarter.

A host of 82,438 in Ohio Stadium saw Coach Woody Hayes' warriors complete Ohio State's first spotless season since 1944 and only its third of all time, with the Rose Bowl still to come.

A cloud of rose perfume filled the press box as the final gun sounded and OSU soared to the zenith by triumph over its oldest, and most feared and respected opponent.

Amid the bedlam, with thousands of fans covering the gridiron, the goal posts toppled in record time.

It will be OSU's third trip to Pasadena for the Rose Bowl. In the first, back in 1921, the Buckeyes were routed, 28-0, by California. In the second, in 1950, they defeated the Golden Bears, 17-14.

This time they meet Southern Cal, already in as the Pacific Coast entry.

Never was a victory more difficult to attain. Without their great right halfback, Bob Watkins, who left with an injury early in the game, the Buckeyes were all but rushed off the field by an alert, determined and resourceful foe.

Straight from the opening kickoff, the underrated Wolverines, their spirit aflame, marched 68 yards for a touchdown, with halfback Dan Cline darting around end untouched seven yards and over.

Big Ron Kramer, the sensational sophomore end, kicked the point.

The Buckeyes continued the post-game celebration inside the locker room with a pre-shower bath.

And for more than 23 minutes of the first half, it continued to be Michigan's game.

Then Jack Gibbs of Columbus, 175-pound second-string fullback — never a regular — seized a flat pass tossed by Jim Maddock, the Michigan quarterback.

Amid the thunder of the great crowd, Gibbs dashed 47 yards to the Michigan 31, before Maddock caught him.

Ohio was penalized five yards for delay, but from 16 yards out, Dave Leggett fired into the end zone to Fred Kriss, a third-string sophomore end.

The left-footed placement of unerring little Thurlow (Tad) Weed made the score 7-7 at the half.

Michigan gained 190 yards, and highly-favored Ohio only 42 in the first half. And the dramatic fight only was beginning.

It was still 7-7 as the last quarter began. The Buckeyes, in an incredible stand, had held Michigan for four downs from the OSU 4-yard line, and then had taken the ball not more than half a yard from their goal stripe.

And from that point a valiant OSU team proved its right to the Big Ten title, the Rose Bowl selection and the national championship.

With Howard (Hopalong) Cassady the thunder-

Third-string sophomore Fred Kriss showed off the Buckeyes' depth with this touchdown catch to tie the score at 7.

bolt, the Buckeyes plowed 99½ yards to take the lead and win the game.

Cassady dashed 52 yards to break the frenzied Wolverine resistance. For the touchdown, from eight yards out, Leggett fired his second scoring pass into the end zone to end Dick Brubaker of Shaker Heights.

Again Weed kicked perfectly and OSU led, 14-7.

The final march came as the All-American Cassady intercepted a Michigan pass by Dan Cline and returned it 13 yards to the OSU 39.

Once more, as so many times this season, the firecracker Ohio running attack overpowered the retiring Wolverines for another 61-yard scoring march.

Cassady bulleted through the line for this one, for a yard away, with just 44 seconds left in the game.

Weed's kick, his 23rd conversion of the season, made the margin 21-7.

There was just time for the kickoff and for Dick Young, a reserve halfback, to intercept another Michigan pass as the game ended.

For a while, the loss of Watkins, OSU's leading ground gainer, seemed devastating.

It forced Coach Woody Hayes to make numerous adjustments in his backfield, particularly with Hubert Bobo, the great sophomore fullback, operating on a bad leg and at one time forced to limp out.

The 82,438 attendance set a new six-game home record for Ohio State, 480,340, and a new all-time record in all games, 642,467.

Even at the finish, Michigan still had the edge in statistics, 15 first downs to 13 and 303 yards of offense against OSU's 254.

Cassady carried 14 times for 94 yards, and Bobo, bad ankle and all, seven times for 52 yards. Leggett made 42 yards in 18 attempts and completed 4 of 9 passes for 58 yards and two touchdowns.

But the interception by Gibbs, the little-used sub, really brought OSU back into the game.

It was the last game in the stadium for the light-weight fullback, one of the 15 seniors who will close their college careers in the Rose Bowl. Gibbs had played only 15 minutes all season.

Hayes, carried off the field by his overjoyed boys, had high praise for everyone.

"In the first half, we were outsmarted, outfought and outplayed," said Hayes. "In the second half, it was the reverse. Cassady's long run and pass interception were the big factors.

"Whenever you go through undefeated, you are lucky. The luck came our way. Our defense was built to stop touchdowns.

"Cassady certainly is an All-American and I will go along with Tom Harmon that he deserves the Heisman.

"It is a real team that can stop Michigan on the 1 and then come back 99 yards for a touchdown. Jim Parker gave us the defensive strength we needed in the clutch.

"I knew Ohio State could not be stopped cold for 60 minutes.

"Jerry Harkrader was outstanding as replacement for Watkins. I will never play him behind Cassady again. Both are back next year and they will be playing at the same time."

In the Michigan dressing room, Coach Benny Oosterbaan congratulated Ohio State.

"We played as well as any time this year," said Oosterbaan. "Ohio is a worthy representative of the Big Ten. I wish them well."

After a Michigan touchdown in the first quarter, Ohio State's defense stood up and shut down the Wolverines the rest of the way.

OHIO STATE WINS NATIONAL CHAMPIONSHIP

Pasadena, Calif., Jan. 1, 1955						
Ohio State	0	14	0	6	–	20
USC	0	7	0	0	–	7

Through mud and driving rain, the Ohio State Buckeyes reached the zenith of the university's football history.

Plowing through the muck and fog in semi-darkness, the Buckeyes vanquished Southern California, 20-7, in the worst weather conditions of Rose Bowl history.

Before 89,191 fans huddled under umbrellas or soaked to the skin, the Buckeyes won their 10th straight game of the season and established their clear claim to the national championship of 1954.

This is the third perfect season in Ohio State's history, and a tremendous achievement for Coach Woody Hayes and his gallant warriors.

After rolling up two touchdowns on their typical impressive power football, the Buckeyes were stunned by a spectacular 88-yard touchdown punt return by Aramis Dandoy, the great senior halfback for the Trojans.

After that, it was a grim, bitter battle through conditions that would have been considered terrible even back in Ohio. The final clinching touchdown came late in the game, as Jerry Harkrader, a junior halfback from Middletown, took a pitchout from quarterback Dave Leggett and sped nine yards around the left side.

Dandoy's touchdown dash was the longest punt return in Rose Bowl history, beating a mark of 62 set by Billy Wells of Michigan State in the Spartans' triumph over UCLA here last year.

Old reliable power football did the job. Despite the slippery, treacherous footing, OSU gained 295 yards rushing.

The Buckeyes led, 14-7, for the first half, and it stayed that way until Harkrader's sprint with 6:41 to play.

The first Buckeye touchdown march of 69 yards in 11 plays was underway near the end of the first

Bob Watkins, the short, powerful OSU halfback, rushed for 67 yards in the Rose Bowl victory over Southern Cal.

quarter. It closed with Leggett sneaking through center, three yards and over, 35 seconds into the second quarter.

This drive was set off by a Trojan fumble recovered by Jim Parker, the huge Buckeye sophomore guard, on the OSU 31, at a moment when the Buckeye situation was precarious.

Tad West kicked the point, and with the score 7-0, OSU struck again in short order. Again it was a recovered fumble that set off the explosion, with Leggett recovering on the Trojan 35.

Bob Watkins, the short, powerful OSU halfback,

burst through the middle for 14, to the 21.

Then Leggett wafted one of his soft passes to Watkins, some five yards from the goal line, and Watkins, side stepping a defender, was over the line. Watkins' kick was good, and OSU led, 14-0, at 2:05 of the second quarter.

At that moment there was every evidence of a

Dave Leggett (with the ball), one of OSU's greatest quarterbacks, was 6-of-11 passing for 65 yards and one touchdown.

rout, as many ardent Big Ten supporters had expected.

But not for long. To say that Dandoy's punt return was like a thunderclap would be an understatement.

The ball was at the OSU 42 and the Buckeyes were forced to kick.

Hubert Bobo, the Buckeye sophomore fullback, who went into this game with an injured knee, got off an amazing kick. There might have been a fumble, but by the time Bobo got the ball, a big Trojan rusher was steaming straight at him.

David Williams (right) and his Buckeye teammates didn't let a little mud get in their way of celebrating a national championship.

Bobo managed to step aside, and then courageously got off his kick anyhow – and it was a beauty.

Dandoy got the ball on his 14 and started upfield with apparently not a chance in the world. Slipping tacklers and bursting through what seemed a cloud of Buckeyes, he emerged in the clear at midfield and was gone.

The sensational spring brought a tremendous roar by the highly partisan crowd.

Sam Tsagalaskis booted the point and it was 14-7, at 9:23 of the second quarter.

Such a climactic run can set afire even an outclassed team, and it did that for the Trojans. From there on it was brutal combat until Harkrader's game-clinching score.

The triumph was one last compliment to one of the greatest OSU backfields ever put together.

Howard (Hopalong) Cassady, in the game practically all the way despite a cracked rib, made 95 yards, Watkins made 67, Harkrader 49 and Leggett 67. Bobo, obviously hobbled by a bad knee, carried only six times for 19 yards.

The biggest ground gainer of the day was Jon Arnett, the fleet sophomore halfback and a track star of the Trojans, with 123 yards in only nine carries.

In total yards gained from scrimmage, it was 360 for OSU and 206 for Southern California.

And the Big Ten is now 8-1 in the Rose Bowl since 1946.

Ann Arbor, Mich., Nov. 19, 1955						
Ohio State	0	3	0	14	–	17
Michigan	0	0	0	0	–	0

BUCKEYES HUMBLE MICHIGAN

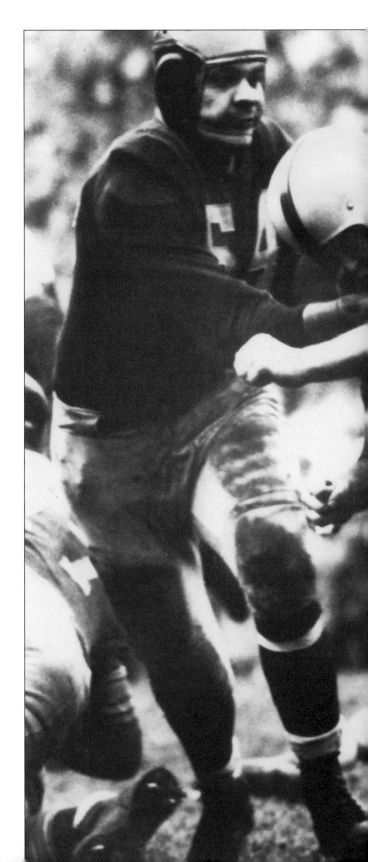

T he most inspiring football team in Ohio State history – a tight-fisted, hard-hitting crew playing the game as it was meant to be played – reigns supreme in the Big Ten for the second year in a row.

In a bone-crunching wallop, led by Howard (Hopalong) Cassady and big Don Vicic, the Buckeye juggernaut today overwhelmed Michigan, 17-0, before 97,369 in Michigan Stadium.

And Ohio State's 13th straight victory, its longest streak ever, puts Michigan State, hated rival of the fallen Wolverines, into the Rose Bowl.

The Spartans, runners-up to OSU for the league

Michigan couldn't stop Jerry Harkrader and the Ohio State ground attack as the Buckeyes piled up a 17-0 victory over the Wolverines.

title, make their second pilgrimage in three years to the classic Tournament of Roses.

It is literally true that the Buckeyes slugged it out with their old foes. The last few minutes of the game were an uproarious donnybrook, with penalties for personal fouls coming so fast it was impossible to keep track of them.

Cassady, the most tremendous OSU ball carrier of all time, closed his amazing career by gaining 146 yards in 28 attempts — 51 yards more than the entire Michigan rushing attack.

Cassady scored one touchdown and fullback Vicic the other, as a fighting Ohio State line shoved Michigan all over its home lot.

The violent warfare reached its climax late in the last quarter, when three successive penalties on Michigan, for personal fouls and unsportsmanlike conduct, landed the ball 18 inches from the Wolverine goal.

From that point Vicic plunged for OSU's second touchdown, at 13:44 of the fourth quarter.

This was Ohio State's first victory over Michigan in Michigan Stadium since 1937, in the era of Buckeyes coach Francis Schmidt 18 years ago — and its fifth all time since the huge bowl opened in 1927.

It was sweet revenge for Michigan's victory over Ohio State in the famed blizzard bowl at Columbus in 1950 — the battle of 47 punts amid disaster conditions that deprived the Buckeyes of a Big Ten title and sent Michigan to the Rose Bowl.

The official attendance of 97,369 was just the number of tickets sold — an all-time record here. Despite five inches of snow in Ann Arbor and more upstate, most of the fans came. Snowbanks decorated the sidelines.

OSU took a 3-0 lead in the second period on a field goal kicked by Fred Kriss from 13 yards out

— a score watched by his delighted father, Howard Kriss, former Cleveland resident and one-time Buckeye star.

The other OSU points, besides the touchdowns, were on a safety in the boisterous last period, when an ill-conceived pass from behind the goal line, Jim Maddock to Terry Barr, found the Michigan receiver smeared behind the goal line by guard Aurelius Thomas and end Bill Michael of the Buckeyes.

Cassady's fourth-quarter touchdown, a dive over center on which he lost the ball after crossing the line and set fire to tense Michigan tempers, was the 37th of his four-year career and his 15th of the season.

In the four seasons, the spectacular Cassady has made 2,466 yards rushing, and with other mileage in all departments, more than 4,500 yards total.

It was another staggering triumph for old-fashioned football — resolute, hard-running and great line play.

The Buckeyes completed only one pass — a 4-yarder from Frank Ellwood to Vicic on the last play of the first half. They tried only three. This was OSU's lone completion in its last three games in victories over Indiana, Iowa and Michigan.

The much ridiculed OSU pass defense drove Michigan crazy, chasing the passer ferociously, intercepting two, and making one Wolverine completion — the one behind the goal line — count for two points.

This was the first time since 1916 and 1917 (in the day of Charles Harley) that Ohio State had won two consecutive Big Ten titles. The Buckeyes won seven straight league games during their perfect record in 1954, and six in a row this season, after losing early season games to Stanford and Duke.

Hayes' Verdict: "Magnificent"

Jubilant over his Ohio State team's 17-0 conquest of Michigan, Buckeye coach Woody Hayes roared praise for his players in the dressing room after the game.

"They were magnificent," said Hayes. "It was the best game I've ever had a team play."

"How many teams hold Michigan scoreless? We beat them for 60 minutes. Our kids played pressure ball for four quarters, I've never seen that done before in my life."

Hayes bubbled over several fine individual performances, but wouldn't single out any player. "It was a great team victory, and they were all magnificent," he said.

Ohio State's first victory at Michigan Stadium since 1937 had Coach Woody Hayes singing with praise after the game.

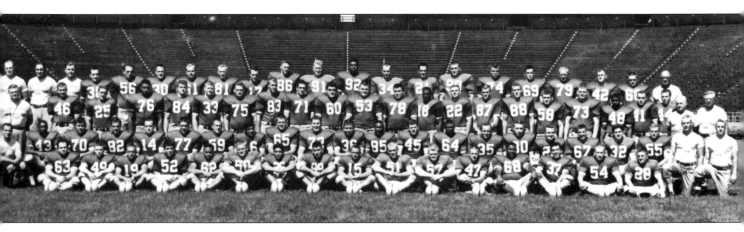

OHIO STATE WINS BIG TEN, EARNS ROSE BOWL BID

Columbus, Nov. 16, 1957						
Iowa	6	0	7	0	–	13
Ohio State	3	7	0	7	–	17

Ohio State's valiant Buckeyes sweep the board of all the Big Ten honors for 1957 and go to the Rose Bowl as undisputed champions of the conference.

Scoring at 11:07 of the final quarter on an awe-inspiring All-America performance by Bob White, the Buckeyes took the title from Iowa, 17-13.

A mighty throng of 82,935, the largest official attendance in the history of Ohio Stadium, saw the Scarlet and Gray miracle men win the Buckeyes' third Big Ten championship – all alone – in the past four seasons.

Surely, Woody Hayes ranks as one of the great coaches in the history of football.

Minus their ace halfback, Don Clark, who did not play at all, the Buckeyes demolished the No.1 defense in the country.

With about eight minutes to go, White started from Ohio State's 32. He blasted through that massive Iowa line seven times in eight plays, for 66 yards. With the ball on the 5, he raged through tackle and over for the winning touchdown with 3:53 to go.

White, gaining 157 yards in 22 attempts, carried the team to its sixth straight Big Ten victory this fall – and Ohio State's 23rd conference triumph in its last 25 games since the start of the 1954 season.

The defeat was the first this year for Iowa, the defending league champion and the Rose Bowl winner over Oregon State last season.

It's true that Ohio State still has a game to play, at Michigan next Saturday – but who cares? The result can't change a thing.

Even without the help of the great Clark, Ohio State gained 332 yards to Iowa's 249. The Buckeyes made 295 running and 37 on two completed passes in 11 attempts.

Iowa had 155 rushing and 94 on nine pass connections in 16 attempts. The tenacious Buckeye defense also had three interceptions.

It will be OSU's third trip to the Rose Bowl. The first, when Wes Fesler was coach, came at the end of the 1949 season, and the Buckeyes defeated California. The second was for the 1955 game, as Ohio State's undefeated national championship team of 1954 defeated Southern Cal.

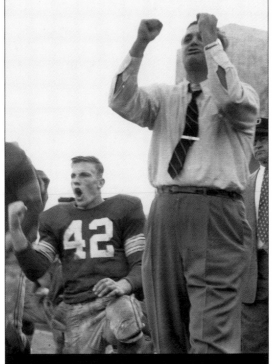

The Buckeyes were fired up after defeating Iowa and earning another trip to California for the Rose Bowl.

The Buckeyes got their first points after only 4:10. They went 73 yards in eight plays, with Don Sutherin kicking a 15-yard field goal.

Iowa came right back with its complicated wide swinging offense and went 66 yards to score a touchdown at 9:50, with end Bob Prescott catching a pass from quarterback Randy Duncan. Prescott missed the point and Iowa led, 6-3.

In the second quarter an Iowa fumble was recovered by end Jim Houston on the OSU 21. The Buckeyes then stormed 79 yards and quarterback Frank Kremblas rammed half a yard through the middle for the touchdown at 6:49 of the second.

Sutherin's conversion made it 10-6 at the half.

But that tricky Iowa offense was still a poisonous problem, with Duncan's passes mixed in with the fast charges of Mike Hagler, Bill Happel, Bill Gravel and John Nocera.

Duncan scored again after a 71-yard march at 9:21 of the third quarter, and with Prescott's kick the Hawkeyes led, 13-10.

There it stood as Ohio State drove deep but failed to score as it was intercepted – by Kevin Furlong – for the first time this season.

That's when, with the clock racing, the Buckeyes finally discovered all they needed was Bob White through the line.

The attendance surpassed the previous official record of 82,881 set in a game with Stanford last year. The unofficial top crowd of 90,000 for the Ohio State-Michigan game here in 1926 was not a definite count and is not recognized by the university.

Don Sutherin, a senior halfback from Toronto, Ohio, kicks the winning 34-yard field goal for Ohio State.

SUTHERIN KICKS OSU TO ROSE BOWL WIN

Pasadena, Calif., Jan. 1, 1958					
Ohio State	7	0	0	3	– 10
Oregon	7	0	0	0	– 7

O hio State's bulldozer Buckeyes are Rose Bowl champions for the third time — but what a struggle it was. Battled to a standstill all the way, the highly-favored Big Ten champions conquered an inspired Oregon team, 10-7.

The slim margin came on a field goal by Don Sutherin, a senior halfback from Toronto, Ohio. It came in the first minute of the last quarter, as the

Buckeyes vs. Oregon, 1958 Rose Bowl

Buckeyes found the underrated Oregon defense almost completely impregnable.

Quarterback Frank Kremblas had the ball on the 24-yard line, and Sutherin — in a tense moment when Ohio State's prestige hung in the balance — booted a bullseye 34 yards between the uprights.

The Buckeyes won, but even an Ohioan must admit that the valiant Ducks gained much of the glory. If ever there has been a "moral victory" this was it — for coach Len Casanova and for a great team that most thought would be a pushover in this game.

It was the second time Ohio State won the Rose Bowl on a field goal. In 1950, the Buckeyes triumphed over California, 17-14, on a placement by Jimmy Hague of Rocky River.

And among other things, Ohio State can thank Sutherin for its splendid record of 1957. It was the same Sutherin who kicked the team to victory over Wisconsin during the regular season — a triumph that helped send the Buckeyes to the Rose Bowl.

But to the throng of 98,202 who nearly filled this fabled stadium — and to the millions of television viewers — the real hero of the day probably was Jack Crabtree, the Oregon quarterback.

Crabtree's forward passes almost — but not quite — struck Ohio State into submission. The nimble and eagle-eye quarterback connected on 10 of 17 passes for 135 yards with two intercepted, both by 172-pound Joe Cannavino of Cleveland.

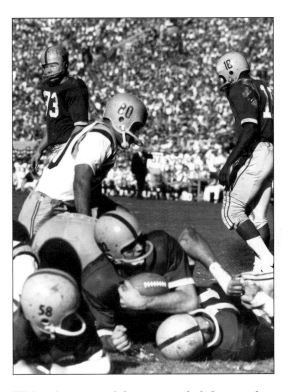

With only two touchdowns scored, defense took center stage at the 1958 Rose Bowl game between Ohio State and Oregon.

Crabtree was voted Player of the Game. Oregon end Ron Stover caught 10 passes for 144 yards.

So it was very close, but at the finish of this searching test the result once more was a victory for solid power football over the forward pass.

Let's give the Buckeyes full credit. For two weeks they were bombarded with the idea that a win was in the bag.

And if it was a bad day for the Buckeyes, they had the courage to hang in there and win.

It was the second Rose Bowl victory for Coach Woody Hayes, whose unbeaten 1954 team defeated Southern Cal here in the 1955 game, 20-7.

Maybe the Buckeyes started too well. From the

Quarterback Frank Kremblas (18) finished off a 79-yard drive with OSU's only touchdown of the day.

opening kickoff they marched 79 yards to score, with Kremblas scoring on a quarterback keeper. The key play on the drive was a 37-yard pass to end Jim Houston.

Everyone had been warned that this was an Ore-gon team with great poise during times of adversi-ty, and the Buckeyes found it alarmingly true.

Taking the ball on their 20 after a punt into the end zone, the daring Ducks boomed 80 yards in 10 plays to tie it up. Jim Shanley, the team's amazing 170-pound halfback, whisked around end for the touchdown, at 2:15 of the second quarter.

Fullback Jack Morris, the Ducks' placement spe-cialist, made it 7-7. After that, it was a grim, fasci-

nating combat, with the Buckeyes often in serious trouble.

"The field goal and the four breaks — two interceptions and two recovered Oregon fumbles — were the only real edge in the game, and we got 'em all," said Hayes.

And Cannavino, the slender halfback from Collinwood, was the hand of fate in these breaks.

In addition to his two interceptions, Cannavino recovered a fumble in the fourth quarter that rescued the Buckeyes.

The Ducks were moving with devastating effect. Crabtree passed to Stover for 23 yards. As he made the catch, Stover was hit hard by end Leo Brown.

The star end dropped the ball and Cannavino dove on it at the Ohio State 24.

Not that this settled everything. With the game almost over and three minutes to play, Oregon was striking again, only to be set back 15 yards on a clipping penalty. The Ducks almost got back this lost yardage, but there was too much to make up.

Ohio State got the ball on downs at mid-field, and Kremblas was piling into the line as it ended.

Oregon with good reason concentrated on Bob

Kremblas tries a quarterback keeper around the right side as the Ohio blockers set up in front of him.

White, the Buckeyes' sophomore fullback who had demolished Iowa and Michigan. Still, White made 104 yards in 25 carries.

Late in the game, Galien Cisco, the Ohio co-captain who had alternated with White, took over the burden in the Buckeyes' last desperate attempt for a second touchdown. Cisco carried seven times in nine plays, including six straight as Ohio drove to the Oregon 36, but then was stopped by the tireless Oregon line. Cisco gained 29 yards in seven attempts.

Oregon (191 passing, 160 running) outgained the Buckeyes, 351 yards to 304. Ohio State had 245 on the ground and 59 passing.

An oddity was that in the third period, Morris, the usually infallible Oregon kicker who had won four games for the Ducks this season, tried and failed on a field goal that would have sent Oregon ahead. This boot was from almost exactly the same spot on the field where Sutherin later succeeded.

After beating Iowa, Woody Hayes said, "You were the greatest football team I ever saw out there today."

BUCKEYES UPSET IOWA'S CHAMPS

Iowa City, Iowa, Nov. 15, 1958						
Ohio State	7	14	7	10	–	38
Iowa	7	14	7	0	–	28

O hio State's embattled Buckeyes, in one of the most amazing comebacks in OSU history, felled mighty Iowa, 38-28. Fullback Bob White galloped 71 yards for one touchdown, scored two others, and personally cracked through Iowa's shattered defense for 209 yards.

Don Clark of Akron, the brilliant senior left halfback, all but equaled White's spectacular feats. Clark raced for 152 yards in only 15 attempts, going 25 yards for one touchdown and 37 yards for another.

70

Clark completely overshadowed Iowa's much-feared pack of fast ball carriers as the aroused and rampant Buckeyes conquered their highly-rated rivals.

After the game, Coach Woody Hayes told his players, "You were the greatest football team I ever saw out there today."

A crowd of 58,643 sat silent and aghast as the Buckeyes scored in the opening minutes and, though tied four times, never were behind.

Going into the game the Hawkeyes had already clinched the undisputed Big Ten title and the Rose Bowl trip. The Hawkeyes finished with a league record of 5-1, with Notre Dame still to play. OSU is 3-2-1 in the league.

Quarterback Randy Duncan of Iowa, one of the finest passers in the land, completed 23 of 33 for 249 yards.

Ohio State threw only two passes, with one of them, Jerry Fields to Jim Houston, going 65 yards to set up one of White's touchdowns on a 1-yard plunge.

Bob White (33) gets carried off the field after he "carried" the Buckeyes with three TDs, including a 71-yard run.

Ohio State gained 397 yards running and 65 passing and Iowa made 178 rushing and 259 passing.

The score was 28-28 going into the final quarter as an Iowa punt went over the goal line.

The Buckeyes took the ball on their 20 and White and Clark faced the Hawkeye defense.

Then began one of the most dramatic winning charges ever seen on a Big Ten gridiron — 80 yards for the decisive touchdown.

In this assault White carried on 11 of 14 plays, including the last six in a row from about 14 yards out.

The onslaught began inauspiciously. Clark was held to two yards on the Ohio 22, and then White was nailed for no gain. On third down, quarterback Fields, replacing the injured Frank Kremblas and playing only his second full game this season, faked a pass and ran 15 yards.

Then White burst for 6, 9, 4 and 23 yards on consecutive plays and carried the Buckeyes to the Iowa 21.

Clark, on an end sweep, added three more and White rammed for five more to the 13. He was held to one yard on the next try and there was a yard left on fourth down. White made it for first down inside the 10.

Then White again surged 7 yards to the 3. Another plunge went to the 1, then the great fullback catapulted over the line for the touchdown.

In two previous trips to Iowa City, in 1952 and 1956, Ohio State had been shut out, 8-0 and 6-0.

71

OHIO STATE PILES IT UP ON MICHIGAN

O hio State ran rampant and registered their biggest point total of all
time against Michigan, 50-20, in 61
years of football warfare since 1897.

The impressive triumph brought
Ohio State an unbeaten record for the season (8-0-
1) and, with Minnesota's loss to Wisconsin, gave the
Buckeyes the undisputed Big Ten title – their fourth
league crown under Woody Hayes.

Ohio State's other championships under Hayes
were in 1954, 1955 and 1957.

It was the Buckeyes' second campaign without
a loss during the 11-year coaching regime of Hayes.
The other was the 10-0 season in 1954.

Bob Ferguson, the Buckeyes' powerful, 217-
pound senior fullback, closed his Big Ten career
impressively. He scored four touchdowns, giving

Ann Arbor, Mich., Nov. 25, 1961						
Ohio State	7	14	0	29	–	50
Michigan	0	6	6	8	–	20

*Bob Ferguson, runner-up for the 1961 Heisman
Trophy, scored four touchdowns against
Michigan.*

him 11 for the season.

The Buckeyes ended with a flourish for their final touchdown, sweeping 80 yards with just 34 seconds to play.

On the kickoff, Ohio State took the ball on its 20. Joe Sparma, a sophomore quarterback from Massillon, tossed a pass to Paul Warfield, and the speedster with the long stride galloped to Michigan's 10 before he was knocked out of bounds by Bill Hornbeck.

Only about 20 seconds remained, but there was time for Sparma to toss three incomplete passes. On the fourth, the target was Sam Tidmore, a 215-pound end from Cleveland whose job is primarily defense.

Tidmore, also a senior in his last conference game, made the catch on the 2 and fought his way over with sheer strength, carrying two desperate Wolverines with him. There were six seconds to play.

Coach Woody Hayes sends halfback Bob Klein, from Athens, Mich., into the game against the Wolverines.

Here Ohio State must have remembered some of the massive scores Michigan had piled up on the Buckeyes in years past, such as 86-0 in 1902, 40-0 in 1940, 45-7 in 1943 and 58-6 in 1946.

Leading, 48-20, the Buckeyes went for the extra two points that would make it 50. Again Tidmore was chosen and caught the conversion pass from Sparma in the end zone.

Ohio State's biggest point total over Michigan had been 38-0 in 1935, when Francis Schmidt coached OSU and Harry Kipke coached Michigan.

The victory gave Ohio State a clean bill in the Big Ten — six straight — and it was the worst defeat of the season for Michigan. The score might have some bearing on the Buckeyes' national ranking, which has been No. 2 to Alabama the last two weeks.

Ohio State quarterback Rex Kern (10) spots wide receiver Jan White (80) open across the middle.

OHIO STATE BLANKS
HIGH-POWERED PURDUE

Columbus, Oct. 12, 1968					
Purdue	0	0	0	0	— 0
Ohio State	0	0	13	0	— 13

Down through the long and proud history of Ohio State football, there have been few times the Buckeyes have been more proud than this.

With one of the all-time great defensive performances, the scarlet and gray gladiators of Coach Woody Hayes rose up to smash the heralded football machine from Purdue, 13-0.

"It was the greatest effort I've ever seen," Hayes declared. "The coaches and the kids did a tremendous job. I can't remember a greater victory than this."

It came before a record crowd of 84,834 in Ohio Stadium, and it came as the result of a superb effort by so many.

Here was Purdue, rated No. 1 in the nation after

three tremendous victories and averaging 41.3 points a game. Purdue was a two-touchdown favorite and few thought an OSU victory was possible.

Time and again the inspired Buckeye offense, led by super sophomore quarterback Rex Kern, hammered its way goalward, only to be thwarted by a penalty or a missed field goal.

The Buckeyes tried three field goals but failed to connect.

This left it up to the defense, led by another one of OSU's super sophs, cornerback Jack Tatum.

After repeatedly blunting the powerful Purdue attack, the first break came on the fourth play of the third quarter. Mike Phipps, Purdue's talented quarterback, was passing from his own 31. He tried to hit end Bob Dillingham in the left flat but defensive halfback Ted Provost was there. He cut in front of Dillingham, plucked the ball out of the sky and raced untouched into the end zone.

Late in the same quarter, Phipps was back again on his own 17. The Buckeye forward wall was applying the heavy pressure, as it had all afternoon. Phipps tried to hit Dillingham again, this time over the middle, but linebacker Jim Stillwagon, a sopho-

Jack Tatum (32) and the Ohio State defense blanked a Purdue offense that averaged 41.3 points per game.

more from Mt. Vernon, was there to pick it off at the Purdue 26.

Five plays later, Buckeye quarterback Bill Long dropped back to pass on a third-and-15. His receivers were covered, so he took off up the middle and scampered 15 yards into the end zone.

Jim Roman's kick was good and the Buckeyes had their triumph.

It was Long's first play of the day. Kern had injured his shoulder on the previous play when he was rolled out of bounds on an option. The injury wasn't serious and Kern did return at the start of the final quarter.

What did Coach Jack Mollenkopf think of all this? "We just got clobbered, that's all. I thought we could get in once or twice but their defense just rose up and stopped us. I guess Woody outcoached me.

"He beat the best Purdue team we've ever had," Mollenkopf added with a slight smile, and then dropped his head.

The tremendous Ohio State defense limited All-American Leroy Keyes to 19 yards on seven carries. Fullback Perry Williams gained 29 on 11 tries.

"I knew we could run against them. Sure, their line is big but it's easy to see," Hayes said.

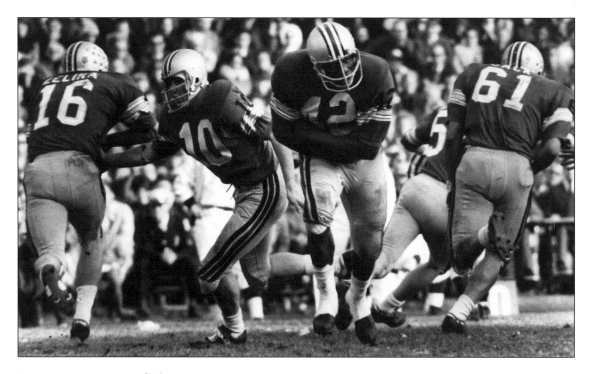

Quarterback Rex Kern (10) and the OSU backfield kept Michigan guessing all afternoon.

ROSE BOWL-BOUND OSU CRUSHES MICHIGAN

Columbus, Nov. 23, 1968						
Michigan	7	7	0	0	–	14
Ohio State	7	14	6	23	–	50

It was Ohio State's finest hour.

The undefeated Buckeyes won the Big Ten title and a trip to the Rose Bowl with an astounding 50-14 victory over Michigan.

A record crowd of 85,370 almost rocked 47-year-old Ohio Stadium off its foundation with thunder-

ous approval as the Buckeyes completely destroyed their most bitter rivals in the game that meant so much.

The Buckeyes took charge in the second quarter and there was no doubt of the outcome, only the size of the score.

Ohio State was quick and devastating on defense, and that's where the issue was decided as the Buckeyes completely throttled Michigan in the second half by holding the explosive Wolverines scoreless. It was one of OSU's most thorough thrashings of Michigan in the series dating to 1897, and the worst drubbing handed to the Wolverines since 1961, when Ohio State romped, 50-20.

It was a great windup to a great season for Coach Woody Hayes and his young and brash sophomores. He started 11 of them — five on offense and six on defense — and they played with the poise of veterans. They blocked crisply and tackled like there was no tomorrow.

The No. 2 Buckeyes, boasting the best defense in the Big Ten, left little doubt that this is truly one of the finest teams to come along in the Big Ten in many years. They played alert, aggressive football and they'll do the conference proud in the Rose Bowl in Pasadena against No. 1 Southern Cal on New Year's Day. The Buckeyes will take a perfect 9-0 record to the West Coast.

It was OSU's 11th undisputed Big Ten title and Hayes' fifth in his 18 seasons in Columbus. Woody

has waited seven years for this day, since 1961, when the Buckeyes last won the conference title but couldn't go to Pasadena because the OSU faculty council overruled the trip. This will be Hayes' fourth trip to the Rose Bowl.

Fullback Jim Otis scored four times to run his season total to 16 touchdowns. Ron Johnson, who scored both of Michigan's TD's, was limited to 91 yards on the ground by the ferocious OSU defense. Johnson had rolled for 347 yards last weekend against Wisconsin.

As the game drew to a close, OSU fans began to celebrate their victory early.

NO. 1 BUCKEYES WHIP TROJANS IN ROSE BOWL

Pasadena, Calif., Jan. 1, 1969						
Ohio State	0	10	3	14	–	27
USC	0	10	0	6	–	16

Ohio State quarterback Rex Kern rolls to his left against a stingy USC defense before a capacity crowd of 102,063 at the Rose Bowl.

Undefeated and unquestionably the nation's No.1 team.

Ohio State's magnificent Buckeyes gave a convincing demonstration that they're the national champions by scoring a decisive 27-16 victory over previously undefeated Southern Cal before 102,063 in the Rose Bowl game.

Coach Woody Hayes' team battled back from a 10-0 deficit to maintain its perfect record in the

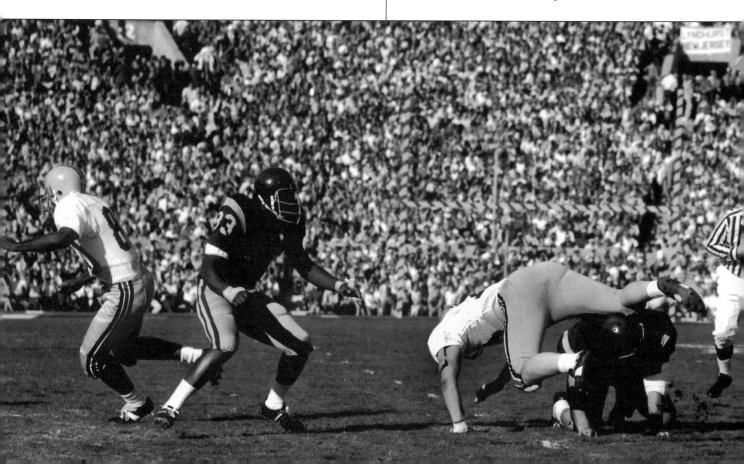

New Year's Day classic.

Hayes has brought three teams to the grand-daddy of all bowl games — in 1955, 1958 and this season — and each time the Buckeyes won.

Actually, it was Ohio State's fourth consecutive triumph in the Rose Bowl because the 1950 team, coached by Wes Fesler, topped Southern Cal, 17-14.

Yesterday's triumph, Ohio State's 10th straight for Hayes' third undefeated season in 18 years, had to be the most satisfying because it was accomplished with a young team (13 sopho-mores in the lineup) and with several players nursing injuries.

Hayes lost senior center John Muhlback of Massillon, who suffered a left leg injury in the fourth quarter, and Cleveland tailback Lar-

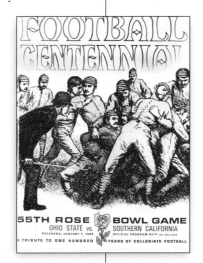

ry Zelina saw action only in the first half. Fullback Jim Otis played with bruised ribs and linebacker Mark Stier had a slight shoulder separation.

Yet, the Buckeyes marshaled their resources, calling on substitute right halfback Ray Gillian to fill in for Zelina, and what a job he did as a pass catch-er. So did tailback Leo Hayden, another sophomore, and the OSU defense, which was brilliant in the second half as it recovered two Trojan fumbles and converted them into scores.

Sophomore quarterback Rex Kern, of Lancaster, Ohio, was named Player of the Game. He completed 9 of 15 passes for 101 yards and two touchdowns.

Heisman Trophy winner O.J. Simpson of South-ern Cal rushed for 171 yards on 28 carries. But only

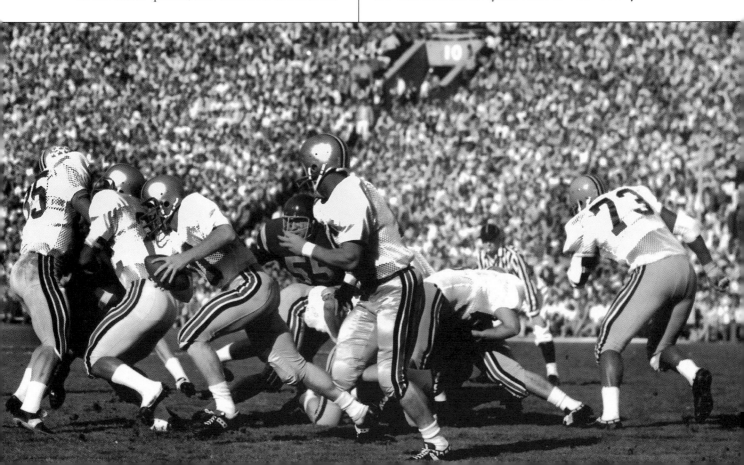

34 of those yards came in the second half as the OSU defense put in a superb effort.

"We were hurting physically, but they got together at halftime and said they were determined not to let O.J. break loose," OSU defensive coordinator Lou McCullough said.

Simpson added one touchdown to his career total of 36 by dashing 80 yards in the second quarter.

It was the same hard-hitting OSU defense that gave the OSU offense opportunities in the second half. Time and again Dave Whitfield, Paul Schmidlin, Jim Sillwagon, Doug Adams and Stier came charging through to nail quarterback Steve Sogge for losses. And twice Sogge fumbled. He also had two passes intercepted — by sophomores Mike Sensibaugh and Tim Anderson.

Sogge, who said he had never faced such a tremen-

dous pass rush, completed 19 of 30 for 189 yards. He salvaged a little pride when he fired a 19-yard TD pass to Sam Dickerson with 45 seconds left in the game, which precipitated a wild ending. Dickerson and OSU's Mike Polaski went up for the ball and it looked like Polaski took it away from the Trojan, but the officials ruled that Dickerson was entitled to a touchdown.

At this point, Hayes stormed out on the field to protest. On the ensuing kickoff OSU was penalized for Hayes' walk on the field, but it mattered little.

After Ohio State battled from a 10-0 deficit to gain a 10-all tie just before intermission, there was no doubt the Buckeyes would get the victory. They tackled hard and were alert.

Jim Roman, who kicked field goals of 26 and 25 yards and booted three extra points, put OSU ahead to stay when he kicked a 25-yarder that broke the tie.

The Buckeyes made it 20-10 when Vic Sottlemeyer recovered Sogge's fumble on the USC 21. Five plays later OSU scored, with Leo Hayden taking a 4-yard pass from Kern.

President-elect Richard Nixon, left, and comedian Bob Hope were among the celebrities in attendance at the Rose Bowl.

Buckeyes coach Woody Hayes shares strategy with quarterback Rex Kern on the sideline during the Rose Bowl.

Ohio State clinched the victory at 10:05 of the final quarter when Simpson fumbled at the USC 21. He was hit by Stier, with Polaski recovering on the 16. With the Trojans blitzing, Kern lofted a touchdown pass to Gillian. Roman kicked the extra point and it was OSU, 27-10.

Otis and Hayden were OSU's workhorses on offense with Otis piling up 101 yards and Hayden 90. Kern had 35 in 12 carries and Gillian was OSU's leading receiver with 69 yards in four catches.

Zelina, before he left the game, had two catches for 14 yards. Simpson was USC's top receiver with 85 yards in three catches.

After a scoreless first quarter, Southern Cal got on the board first following a missed field goal by Ohio State.

The Buckeyes marched from their 38 to the USC 10, but Zelina's field-goal attempt was wide left.

Zelina's try was the first play of the second quarter. The Trojans then drove to the OSU 3. Ohio State's Jack Tatum caught Simpson at the 3 following Simpson's 16-yard reception from Sogge.

Here Ohio State's defense braced. Simpson was stopped for no gain of the first play. On second down, Simpson ran into a stone wall again and lost a yard as Mike Sensibaugh and Tim Anderson hit him. Now it was third down, and it was here the Trojans reached into their bag of tricks. Sogge pitched out to Simpson, who fired a pass that was overthrown for Terry Dekraai in the end zone.

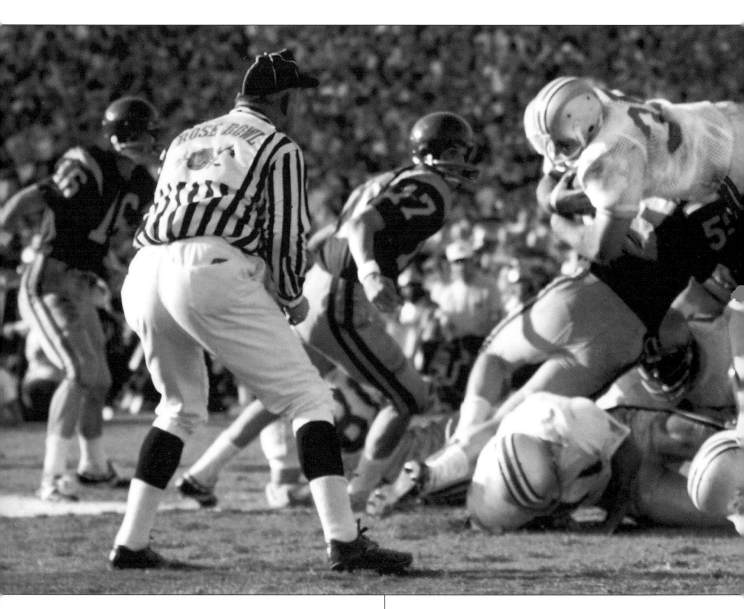

The Buckeyes put the game away — and won the national championship — thanks to two fourth-quarter touchdowns.

Now the Trojans had one down left and they sent in Ron Ayala, who booted a 21-yard field goal. The time was 9:40.

On the ensuing kickoff, the Buckeyes were stopped after making one first down at midfield and punted. Simpson then electrified the crowd by romping 80 yards through for USC's first touchdown. It came at 8:20 and it was the second longest play from scrimmage in the Rose Bowl. Ayala booted the extra point and the Trojans were off and running.

BUCKEYES VS. SOUTHERN CAL, 1969 ROSE BOWL

However, the Buckeyes refused to fold. They bounced back and went 69 yards in 13 plays when Otis plunged in from the 1. The big gainer in this drive was an 18-yard pass from Kern to Ray Gillian.

Gillian, replacing the injured Zelina, made a sensational grab as he leaped high for the pass at the USC 3. After Otis made 2 yards on a smash over cen-ter, Kern again gave the ball to the junior fullback and he scored. Jim Roman kicked the extra point.

The Buckeyes tied the score at 10-all when they covered 60 yards with 1:04 left amd Roman kicked a 26-yard field goal. On the drive, Kern again went to the air, hitting end Jan White for 17 and Gillian for 19 as the precious seconds ticked off.

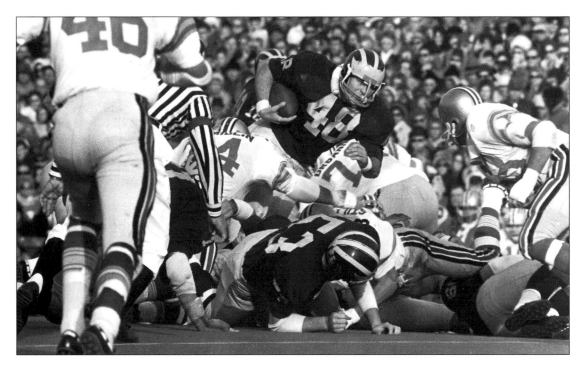

U-M fullback Garvie Craw tries the middle of the Ohio State defense for a 3-yard gain in the third quarter.

SCHEMBECHLER UPSETS MENTOR HAYES

Ann Arbor, Mich., Nov. 22, 1969					
Ohio State	6	6	0	0	– 12
Michigan	7	17	0	0	– 24

A record college football crowd of 103,588 witnessed one of the great upsets of all time when Michigan's inspired Wolverines stunned No. 1 Ohio State, 24-12, to gain a share of the Big Ten title and sew up an invitation to the Rose Bowl.

It was a great day for the Wolverines, who entered the game 15-point underdogs. But they didn't play like underdogs. They beat Ohio State with a first-half punch, scoring all their points in the first half, and then resorted to a brilliant defense by intercepting six OSU passes and playing aggressive hard-charging football.

It was a big day for first-year Coach Bo Schembechler — the genius pupil who beat his old mentor — Woody Hayes. Schembechler learned his lessons many years ago when he coached under Hayes at OSU.

Schembechler and his staff conceived a brilliant defense to shut off OSU's running attack and stymie its passing game.

"We can't lay an egg today. We have come to win," Schembechler declared before the game. But few in the mammoth bowl of Michigan Stadium and millions in the television audience would have believed him. But Schembechler was a believer. He believed in himself, and most of all, he believed in his team, which is stacked with 21 Ohioans.

All of them performed, but defensive back Barry Pierson, who made a 60-yard punt return to pave the way for one Michigan touchdown and intercepted three passes, has to be singled out as one of the big stars.

There were others — captain and end Jim Mandich of Solon, safety Tom Curtis of Aurora, the Michigan offensive and defensive lines, and the backfield, headed by quarterback Don Moorhead and fullback Garvie Craw, who scored three touchdowns between them. The 218-pound Craw scored twice on short runs and Moorhead once on a 2-yard burst.

Tim Killian kicked a 25-yard field goal for Michigan's other score. He missed four other field-goal attempts — of 47, 39 and 43 yards in the third quarter, and one of 46 yards in the fourth. But those points weren't needed because OSU could not generate much offense in the second half.

Fullback Jim Otis and end Jan White tallied for Ohio State in the first half. Otis went in from 1 yard and White took a 22-yard pass from Rex Kern, who had four passes intercepted and hit 6 of 17 for 88 yards.

His replacement, Ron Maciejowski of Bedford, hit only 3 of 10 and had two picked off.

It was a bitter setback for Ohio State, which only once penetrated past midfield in the second half, and for Hayes, who saw an unbeaten season, and second straight national and Big Ten titles go down the drain. Hayes had to settle for a share of the crown — his sixth since coming to OSU 19 years ago.

The loss was OSU's first after eight victories this season and snapped a 22-game winning streak dating to 1967. OSU also failed in its bid for a record 18th straight Big Ten victory. The Buckeyes now have won 17 straight conference games twice — during the 1954-55-56 seasons, and from 1967 through yesterday.

Hayes had only praise for Michigan, which out-rushed OSU, 266 to 22, but yielded in passing yards to the Buckeyes, 155-108.

Michigan also had a slight edge in first downs, 21-20, in what was a bruising display of defense on the part of the Wolverines.

Michigan twice came from behind in the first half, and that was the tipoff that it was ready to spring an upset.

Michigan played Ohio State off its feet in the first half as the Wolverines refused to be impressed with OSU's No. 1 rating or its unbeaten record. Michigan succeeded in doing what eight other teams were unable to do — run with consistency and pass equally well.

Kern was under great pressure by a fast-charging Wolverine defense and the Buckeye running attack also sputtered.

BUCKEYES GET REVENGE

Columbus, Nov. 21, 1970					
Michigan	0	3	6	0	— 9
Ohio State	3	7	0	10	— 20

Ohio State, keyed to an unbelievable emotional pitch, won the Big Ten championship with an impressive 20-9 victory over Michigan.

In full view of a national television audience and a record Ohio Stadium crowd of 87,331, Woody Hayes' Buckeyes gained full revenge for last year's defeat at Ann Arbor — their only blemish on a glorious three-year record of 31 victories in 32 games.

In dominating Michigan with a fierce second-half defense, the Buckeyes won their 12th Big Ten title and Hayes' sixth in 20 years.

They finished with a 9-0 record, 7-0 in the conference, and go to the Rose Bowl as undisputed Big Ten champion to face Stanford.

It was a gratifying moment for Hayes and his squad. It was evident in the second half that this was their day as the OSU defense time and again responded with clutch plays.

Michigan, which came into the game with impressive credentials and boasted a potent offense that averaged 31 points a game in nine straight victories, could not overcome OSU's bulldozer attack and defense, which limited the Wolverines to just 37 yards on the ground.

John Brockington, the bulldozer fullback, finds an opening in the Michigan defense. He finished with 77 yards.

Hayes was very proud of the defense and said so after the game. And so was Lou McCullough, Hayes' top lieutenant and defensive coordinator, who spent a full year designing a defense that would stop the vaunted Wolverine attack.

All-American linebacker Jim Stillwagon

"I've been waiting for this moment a whole year," McCullough declared. "They get only one touchdown, only one touchdown. What a job," he said.

There were defensive heroes aplenty, starting with All-American linebacker Jim Stillwagon, who inspired the defense. The 225-pound senior from Mt. Vernon keyed on stopping Michigan quarterback Don Moorhead and he decked the Wolverine ace twice during crucial times of the second half. Stillwagon finished with 12 tackles.

Ohio State running back Leo Hayden plows off-tackle against an aggressive Michigan defense en route to a big gain.

Linebackers Doug Adams and Stan White, tackles Shad Williams and George Hassenhorf, ends Mark Debevc and Ken Luttner, and defensive backs Jack Tatum, Harry Howard, Tim Anderson and Mike Sensibaugh also shared in the tremendous effort.

Moorhead, who set Michigan career records of passes (199) and passing yards (2,540) could not elude OSU's line. He finished 12 of 26 for 118 yards.

The list of offensive stars for OSU begins with quarterback Rex Kern, whose ballhandling magic and timely passing was a key factor in the big victory.

So was the running of halfback Leo Hayden of Dayton, who scored on a 4-yard pitchout in the fourth quarter. He wound up with 117 yards in 28 carries.

John Brockington, the bulldozer fullback from Brooklyn, N.Y., had his moments as the 220-pound senior finished with 77 yards in 27 smashes.

Kern's near-flawless ballhandling pleased Hayes.

"Rex sure had a great day," said Woody. "He was something out there. He was on target, wasn't he?"

The Buckeyes recovered the opening kickoff, which was fumbled by Lance Scheffler on the Wolverine 25. Six plays later, Fred Schram kicked a 28-yard field goal.

Michigan seized a break late in the first quarter when safety Jim Betts intercepted Kern and returned to the OSU 18. Dana Coin's 31-yard field goal tied the game at 3-3.

After the game, Woody Hayes is congratulated by a large gathering of Buckeye fans.

Ohio State put it all together late in the second quarter, moving 47 yards for a TD as Kern, Brockington and Hayden shouldered the load. Kern turned a crucial fourth-and-2 on the Michigan 29 into a first down. Kern faked a handoff to Brockington and kept the ball for a 4-yard gain to the 25.

Three plays later, Kern fired a 26-yard touchdown pass to Bruce Jankowksi, who ran a post pattern as he beat Bruce Elliott. The TD came with 1:18 remaining, and then Schram converted.

The Buckeyes then recovered a Michigan fumble on the Wolverine 24, and as the seconds ticked off they reached the Michigan 23, where confusion developed.

It appeared Kern wanted to throw a pass out of bounds, but Schram came on the field, probably on order from Hayes, and this confused the Buckeyes as the half ended.

Michigan drove 50 yards early in the third quarter to get back in the game as Moorhead took to the air and moved the Wolverines to the OSU 13. On second down, Moorhead fired a cross pattern pass for the score to Paul Staroba as the Michigan split end had to beat only one man, Tim Anderson.

On the extra point try, Coin's kick was blocked by Anderson, who came charging through. Anderson was almost offside on the play.

That preserved Ohio's lead, 10-9.

The Buckeyes had to settle for another field goal early in the fourth quarter. This time Schram kicked a 27-yarder to climax a 74-yard march, giving OSU a 13-9 lead.

Seconds later OSU scored again after linebacker Stan White of Kent, Ohio, intercepted Moorhead and returned the ball to the Michigan 9. Two plays later, Kern flipped to Hayden on an option sweep to the right and Hayden went in easily. Schram converted and OSU had all the points it needed.

Heisman Trophy winner Jim Plunkett gets stacked up at the OSU 1-yard line in the fourth quarter.

STANFORD STUNS OSU

Pasadena, Calif., Jan. 1, 1971						
Stanford	10	0	3	14	–	27
Ohio State	7	7	3	0	–	17

The sharpest shooter in the West, and maybe, in the whole world. That's Stanford's great quarterback, Jim Plunkett.

The Heisman Trophy winner and holder of every NCAA offensive record in the books shot down Ohio State, 27-17, before 103,389 in the 57th Rose Bowl.

Calm, cool and poised all afternoon, Plunkett riddled the Buckeyes with his pinpoint passing, and in the process gave Stanford its first Rose Bowl victory since 1940.

It was a hard-earned victory for Stanford, which came into the game as 10-point underdogs, as Plunkett and his teammates ambushed the Buckeyes with surprising ease in the second half.

Trailing 14-10 at halftime, Stanford stormed back with a Rose Bowl-record 48-yard field goal by Steve Horowitz in the third quarter and two touchdowns in the final quarter to hand the Buckeyes their first defeat after four straight victories in the Rose Bowl.

The go-ahead touchdown came on a 1-yard run by Jackie Brown early in the final quarter, and then Plunkett fired a 10-yard pass to flanker Randy Vataha late in the final quarter to clinch the decision.

Plunkett, voted the game's Most Valuable Player, idled OSU's defenses by completing 20 of 30 passes for 265 yards.

As expected, Ohio State ran almost at will with the ball, rushing for 364 yards, but the Buckeyes couldn't make the big third-down play and three times failed to convert on fourth down deep in Stanford territory.

The OSU pass defense was too lax and often uninspired, which contributed to the Buckeyes' defeat. Stanford dominated the entire second half, its defense being more aggressive.

OSU's defense, superb during its drive for the Big Ten title this season, had a letdown and the Buckeye passing game was ineffective. Quarterback Rex Kern, who scrambled OSU to a 14-10 first-half lead with his running, completed only 4 of 13 passes and had one intercepted.

Ron Maciejowski, his able understudy from Bedford, Ohio, hit on only 3 of 6 and Rick Galbos, a sophomore wingback from Mentor, missed on one rollout attempt after faking a run. So all told, Ohio's passing game made 75 yards on seven completions in 20 tries.

With the defeat, OSU's chances for a possible

Stanford receiver Bob Moore reaches high to make a catch between OSU defenders Tim Anderson (left) and Mike Sensibaugh.

national title went down the drain since No. 1 ranked Texas was upset by Notre Dame. Also scuttled was OSU's unbeaten record, which ended at nine in a row.

Freshman Archie Griffin showed the Ohio State homefolks a glimpse of the future with a record-setting game against North Carolina. Griffin set a school record with 239 yards before 86,180 at Ohio Stadium.

FRESHMAN GRIFFIN RUNS TO RECORD 239 YARDS

Columbus, Sept. 30, 1972					
N. Carolina	7	0	0	7	–	14
Ohio State	3	6	14	6	–	29

Add the name of Archie Griffin to Ohio State's list of instant heroes.

Griffin, an unheralded freshman from Columbus Eastmoor High, almost singlehandedly led Ohio State to a 29-14 victory over previously unbeaten North Carolina in Ohio Stadium.

A standing-room crowd of 86,180 witnessed his-tory on this sunny but cool afternoon as the 5-10, 185-pound Griffin rushed for an OSU-record 239 yards. Griffin eclipsed the old record of 229 yards by Ollie Cline in 1945 against Pitt.

Griffin saved what could have been a disastrous

A familiar sight: Archie Griffin outrunning the North Carolina defense.

day because the Buckeyes, who had two weeks to prepare for the Tar Heels, started badly. Their offense sputtered the first time they had the ball and they were forced to punt.

The second time OSU had the ball it was stopped again. But this time Gary Lago's punt was blocked by sophomore Jerry DeRatt and the ball was recovered on the goal line by Gene

Brown for a North Carolina touchdown.

But then Griffin entered the game. He changed the OSU fans' groans into cheers by carrying three times for 18 yards, and although OSU had to punt again, Griffin offered a new life.

Before the half was over Griffin had 111 yards in 16 carries and the fifth-ranked Buck-eyes, now 2-0 on the season, took a 9-7 lead into halftime.

There was no stopping Griffin in the second half as he sparked three long TD drives by grinding out

128 more yards. He also made one key reception for 17 yards that helped the Buckeyes to a second-quarter TD.

Griffin scored once on a dazzling 9-yard run, which gave OSU a 23-7 lead in the fourth. He darted for the left sideline and tight-roped the out-of-bounds line, doing a jitter step just as he hit the end zone.

Griffin, an 18-year-old who was football, track and wrestling captain at Eastmoor High, where he was voted the 1971 "Back of the Year" in Ohio, was somewhat befuddled by all the attention given him after the game.

"I wasn't aware I needed 15 yards to break the old record," Griffin said outside the OSU locker room as he was surrounded by well-wishers. "I wasn't even aware that I was close to it."

Griffin who made 27 trips to gain his big total, which included a 55-yard scamper, credited OSU's offensive line for his super performance. "They did a hell of a job blocking for me," he said.

When asked if his 239 yards was a personal high for him, he said no. "Once in a high school game I gained 280 yards," he said.

Ohio State coach Woody Hayes revealed that the reason he didn't use his fullbacks Saturday (three had 15 tries for 54 yards) was because North Carolina came out with an eight-man line.

"And when they throw an eight-man front at you it's going to be hard to run," he said, "so we tried other things."

Hayes was impressed with Griffin.

"Archie spoke for himself today," Hayes said. "What is it that makes players that good? I don't know."

Hayes said freshmen are revolutionizing college football. "They give you a bigger squad to work with and show a great deal of where the fine coaching really is – in high schools.

"Take Archie, all you have to do is hand him the ball and he does it. He has power for his 185 pounds, speed and a definite sense of timing.

"I have never been for or against the freshman rule, but Archie tends me to change my mind."

While Griffin supplied most of the fireworks, Ohio State received an excellent running game from Elmer Lippert, a 5-7 junior from Sandusky, who rushed for 116 yards in 10 tries.

Quarterback Greg Hare handled the team well. He completed 5 of 12 passes for 96 yards, and ran for another 20.

Wingback Rich Galbos, co-captain from Mentor, was Hare's top receiver with three catches for 72 yards. Overall, the Buckeyes romped for 526 yards, while Carolina gained 239 rushing and passing.

Hare also scored one TD, romping 17 yards behind great downfield blocking after the Buckeyes' linebacking ace, Randy Gradishar, intercepted a pass to set up the drive.

Fullbacks Randy Keith and Hal (Champ) Henson scored the other OSU TD's. Keith went 11 yards off right guard early in the third and Henson plunged for 1 yard later in that quarter to give OSU a 23-7 edge.

Then Griffin added his TD on a 9-yard scamper and North Carolina scored in the last two seconds of the game when quarterback Nick Vidnovic fired a 37-yard pass to Earle Bethea, but the game was long decided.

OSU's defense, led by co-captain and tackle George Hassenhorl of Garfield Heights, was outstanding again. It held the high-scoring Tar Heels, who came into the game averaging 31 points, scoreless because the one touchdown came when OSU had a punt blocked.

"We played a great defensive game," said Hassenhorl. "We stopped their big plays."

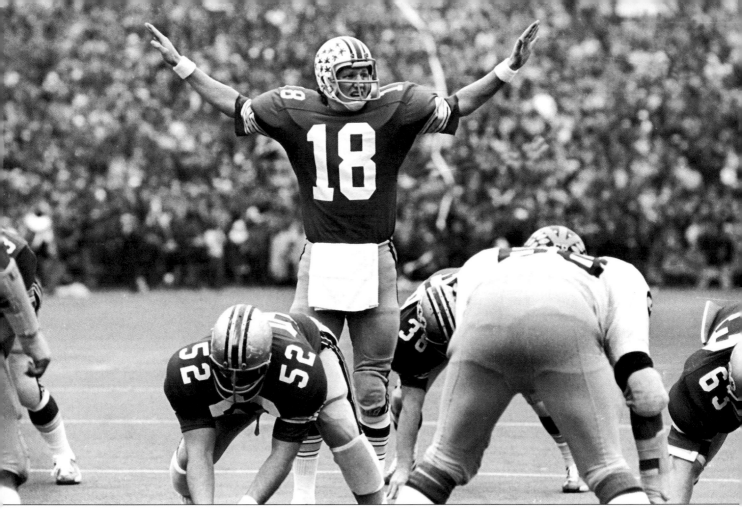

OSU quarterback Greg Hare asks for a little quiet as he brings the troops to the line of scrimmage.

IT'S OFF TO ROSE BOWL
FOR VICTORIOUS OSU

Columbus, Nov. 25, 1972					
Michigan	0	3	8	0 —	11
Ohio State	0	7	7	0 —	14

I t's off to the Rose Bowl and a shot at all the glory for Ohio State.

Reaching into their well of miracles, the Buckeyes defeated favored Michigan, 14-11, in one of the most dramatic and thrilling finishes in Big Ten football history.

Ohio State's superb goal-line defense won this one by turning back Michigan just inches from the end zone and ruining the visitors' bid for a perfect season and trip to Pasadena. It also snapped Michigan's 15-game league winning streak with its first regular-season loss in two years.

So it's Ohio State that will be spending the holidays in California and not Michigan, although the Wolverines had plenty of chances to win or tie the game and couldn't. All Michigan needed was a tie, but it never considered kicking a field goal when it was so close to scoring.

"I never considered it. I didn't want a tie. We wanted to win," said Michigan coach Bo Schembechler, who has a 2-2 record against Ohio State's Woody Hayes.

Hayes, dean of Big Ten coaches in his 22nd year, now has his eighth league title, second co-title, and it has to rank as one of the most satisfying in view of OSU's sticky goal-line defense.

The Buckeyes, finishing the regular season with a 9-1 record and 7-1 in the Big Ten, were outplayed and the statistics prove it with Michigan rolling up 344 yards to OSU's 192, and the Wolverines having 83 plays to 44 for the Bucks.

Harry Banks, who replaced Chuck Heater after the Wolverines had intercepted an OSU pass early in the final quarter and seemed headed for the winning points, carried three straight times with Michigan having a first-and-goal at the OSU 5.

With about a foot to go, Michigan quarterback Dennis Franklin, who just before the half had fumbled on the Buckeye 1, ending a Wolverine drive, was stopped trying to slice his way over center.

The Buckeyes swarmed all over the Massillon, Ohio, sophomore and took over on the 1, and finally punted out of danger.

Michigan had two more chances to get on the scoreboard, one on the next series. The Wolves had great field position, starting at the OSU 37, but failed to make ground on two rushing plays and two passes — one on fourth down with sub Larry Cipa trying to find Heater deep.

The Buckeyes, still nursing a 14-11 lead, had five minutes and 10 seconds to kill on the clock

before they could start celebrating. They made two first downs as they drove to the Michigan 29 when the drive bogged down and little Brian Conway missed a 47-yard field goal.

Michigan took over with 1:20 to play, starting on its 20. Three first downs later, it reached the OSU 41 and its last chance ended as Franklin was nailed by tackle George Hassenhorl at the line of scrimmage, and 13 seconds showed on the clock.

Thousands of Buckeye fans poured onto the field as the south goal post came tumbling down. A little while later, the north post tumbled, despite efforts of 12 policemen to keep order.

Michigan took the lead in the first period on a 35-yard field goal by left-footed Mike Lantry, the 24-year old Vietnam veteran who kicked the Wolverines to victory over Purdue last week.

The Buckeyes, who ran the ball for just six plays from scrimmage in the opening period, pushed ahead, 7-3, on a 1-yard plunge by fullback Champ Henson, which climaxed a 46-yard, eight-play march. Conway kicked the extra point.

Michigan, which controlled the ball for 11 minutes and 23 seconds in the opening quarter, went to work in an effort to take the lead just before the intermission. The Wolverines started on their 20 and moved to the OSU 1 in just eight plays. A 35-yard pass from Franklin to Paul Seal and a 14-yard pass to Clint Haselrig were the big gainers, sandwiched by Heater's fine runs.

With a first-and-goal at the OSU 1, there seemed to be little doubt the Wolverines would score, but the Buckeyes had other plans. Heater took a pitchout and tried going left, only to lose a yard. Then he carried again and slipped two feet from the goal line as 28 seconds remained.

Bob Thornbladh hit the center of the line and was stopped, and suddenly it was fourth down. After

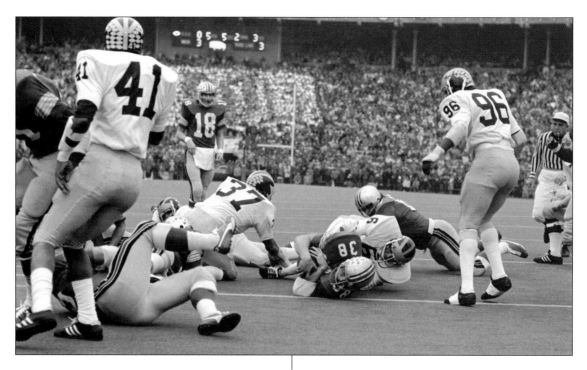

The Buckeyes were beaten on the stat sheet, but not on the scoreboard, ending the Wolverines' travel plans to California.

a timeout, Franklin botched up a snap from center and fumbled, and OSU recovered on the 2 with only seven seconds remaining.

OSU ran one play, Hare falling on the ball after the snap, and the half ended with the Buckeyes leading, 7-3.

Ohio State struck quickly after taking the second half kickoff and marched 78 yards to hike its lead to 14-3 on some fancy running by freshman tailback Archie Griffin, who carried five straight times. Griffin traveled the final 30 yards on a brilliant dash.

Michigan, determined as ever, was not denied the next time it got its hands on the ball. The Wolverines drove to the OSU 5, and with a fourth-

and-inches to go, fullback Ed Shuttlesworth went over right guard for the score to cap the 57-yard drive.

The Wolverines went for two and succeeded as Franklin hit Haselrig to narrow the gap to 14-11.

Then came the frantic final quarter.

Michigan was knocking on the touchdown door twice early in the fourth quarter and both times it was denied. Shuttlesworth, the 235-pound junior from Cincinnati, was stopped on the OSU 1 when he ran into linebacker Rick Middleton, which ended that bid.

A costly OSU interception, with Randy Logan picking off Hare's pass, gave Michigan another opportunity. The Wolverines took over on the OSU 29 and nine plays later were stopped again when Franklin ran into a stone wall on fourth down.

The Buckeyes put up another sterling defensive stand when Michigan moved to the OSU 37, but a fourth-down pass to Heater was low.

Way To Go, Coach Woody

The victory over Michigan was revenge for Woody, after the Buckeyes lost the year before in Ann Arbor.

It was late in the fourth quarter and Ohio State, while trying to protect its 14-11 lead, surprised everyone, including Michigan, by throwing a little swing pass. It was only the third pass the Buckeyes threw all game – and this unexpected one worked.

"Way to go, Woody," yelled a fan near the Ohio State bench.

The cheer was richly deserved.

This was a Woody Hayes victory, one he wanted perhaps more than any other in his long career at Ohio State. He lost the game to Michigan last year that rankled every bone in his aging, fighting body, and the frustration forced him to throw a tantrum that caused him to be roundly spanked here, there and almost everywhere.

He waited a long time to wash away the bitter taste of defeat – and he did it Saturday at packed Ohio Stadium the way it should be done ... with intelligence and emotion, controlled emotion.

Today we give The Old Man full credit. He got his team up to the right pitch. Had he brought them in too high the Buckeyes would have lost. It was a day on which they didn't dare make a major mistake. If anything, I had the suspicion that Michigan was a bit too emotionally keyed, and this intangible perhaps made the difference.

Michigan is a fine team, well coached, and it obviously had more offensive weapons than Ohio State. Had the Wolverines elected to use more short passes they could have won.

This was an upset. Woody and his players served it. Hayes, who wasn't afraid to gamble on a pass in the closing minutes while protecting a lead – even though one of the two previous passes thrown by the Buckeyes had been intercepted – showed a new face, a controlled face, a shrewd face, and his players reflected his disposition.

Way to go, Woody.

99

MICHIGAN, OSU TIE FOR BIG TEN TITLE

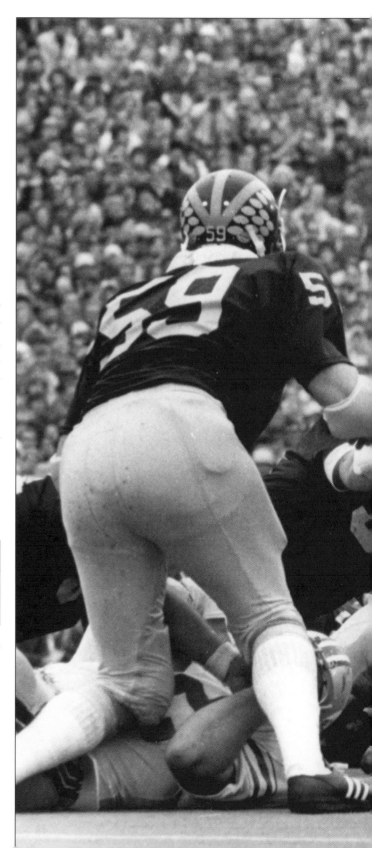

O hio State and Michigan share the Big Ten football title for the second straight year and for the fifth time in the 70-year history of this great series after playing to a 10-10 tie before a record crowd of 105,223.

The identity of the conference's entry in the Rose Bowl won't be known officially until today, but undoubtedly Michigan will be the choice.

The underdog Wolverines, who haven't lost a game in Michigan Stadium in four years, spotted the No. 1 Buckeyes a 10-0 first-half lead and then

Ann Arbor, Mich., Nov. 24, 1973					
Ohio State	0	10	0	0	– 10
Michigan	0	0	0	10	– 10

Big Pete Johnson finds an opening in the middle of the Michigan defense during the Buckeyes' Big Ten finale in Ann Arbor.

100

rallied with a field goal and a touchdown in the fourth quarter to maintain their perfect home slate of going unbeaten in 29 games.

Missed field goals of 58 and 43 yards by Mike Lantry in the last minute of play denied Michigan a victory as the Wolverines took the momentum away from the Buckeyes in the second half and dominated the action.

So now Michigan and Ohio are co-champs again, each team finishing the Big Ten season 7-0-1. The Wolverines ended 10-0-1 overall and Ohio State 9-0-1.

The conference athletic directors decide who will go to the Rose Bowl. The vote was taken after the game, according to Ed Weaver, OSU associate athletic director, and the announcement will be made at 1 p.m. today in Chicago by Big Ten commissioner Wayne Duke. "In the event of a tie vote of the directors, the team that went last will step aside," Duke said.

Since the Buckeyes went last Jan. 1, Michigan would go this time.

Weaver was asked how he voted, "I wish I could tell you, but I can't," he said. "I think you can guess how I voted."

Ohio State coach Woody Hayes, who said his team was emotionally ready for this, its big test of the season, looked and sounded dejected in a post-game interview. He could barely be heard by the throng of writers.

"I guess you'd say we won the first half and they the second," Hayes said while looking at the floor. "I can't consider a tie satisfactory."

Hayes said his team did not make mistakes, "but they (Michigan) ran well on us and they passed out of tough situations. We didn't pass earlier because our passing is not very good."

Hayes now has nine Big Ten titles in 23 years (six outright and three shares).

Michigan coach Bo Schembechler, bagging his fourth conference title — third co-championship — said his team played a great second half and deserved to win.

"They have character and they fought and came back," Bo said. "I'm extremely proud of them. We didn't settle for a tie, we did everything we could to win."

Schembechler said his team deserves to be in the Rose Bowl.

What was Hayes' opinion on the subject?

"I have no opinion on the Rose Bowl," Hayes said. "I have nothing to say. If we're selected we'll go."

U-M Coach Bo Schembechler calls the decision to send Ohio State to Pasadena "tragic" after hearing the news.

BUCKEYES VS. MICHIGAN, 1973

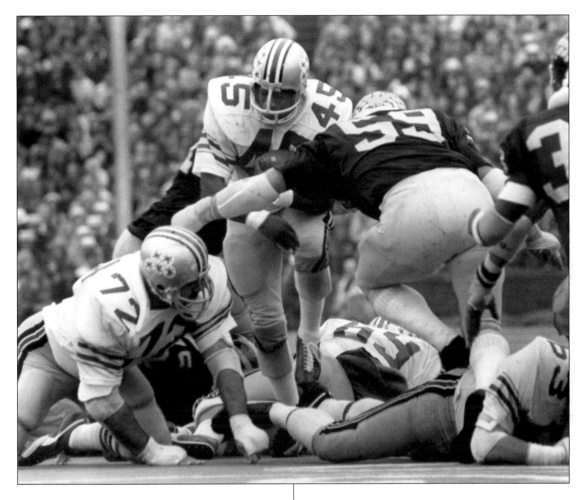

The Michigan defense focused much of its attention on stopping Buckeye running back Archie Griffin (45).

Hayes, who turned 60 this year, was asked how he would rate the 1973 Buckeyes.

"I still have to go back to the 1968 Rose Bowl team. They won them all. You have to win them all," he said.

Hayes said tailback Archie Griffin, who rushed for 165 yards in 30 carries, was the greatest back on the field, and not many here or among the millions watching on television would dispute that claim.

Quarterback Dennis Franklin, a junior from Massillon, and fullback Ed Shuttlesworth were Michigan's key performers.

Franklin's timely passing moved the Wolverine attack. Shuttlesworth was a hard runner to stop. The big fullback from Cincinnati powered the Michigan offense with 116 yards in 27 carries for a 4.2-yard average.

Franklin, who rushed for only 17 yards, hit 7 of 11 passes for 99 yards. His fourth-quarter passing paved the way for Michigan to score the tying touchdown.

103

BUCKEYES ROUT USC, 42-21

O hio State vindicated the Big Ten's athletic directors, and gained a measure of revenge themselves, with a 42-21 triumph over Southern Cal in the 60th Rose Bowl.

The Big Ten carried a four-game losing streak in the Rose Bowl into this contest, including last year's humiliating 42-17 loss by the Buckeyes against this same USC team.

Ohio State won in impressive style. It ran the ball well — as expected — and it passed unexpectedly well.

The timely passing of sophomore quarterback Cornelius Greene and the brilliant running of tailback Archie Griffin were the chief ingredients as Ohio State scored 28 points in the sec-

Pasadena, Calif., Jan. 1, 1974						
Ohio State	7	7	13	15	–	42
USC	3	11	7	0	–	21

Pete Johnson goes airborne and sails into the end zone for one of his three touchdowns.

105

ond half to break a 14-14 tie.

Greene, voted the Most Valuable Player of the game, set up two touchdowns with his passing and scored the go-ahead TD late in the third quarter on a 1-yard run after Neal Colzie's 56-yard punt return.

Greene finished 6 of 8 passing for 129 yards.

Griffin, the brilliant sophomore, had his 11th straight 100-yards plus game rushing. The 184-pound All-American rambled for 149 yards in 22 carries. He capped a hard day's work by scoring the last TD of the game, a dazzling 47-yard run late in the final quarter.

"We've never been this good in a Rose Bowl game," said OSU coach Woody Hayes. "Any team that wins by three touchdowns over Southern Cal has to be good."

Hayes then talked about a subject he rarely brings up — passing.

"We worked 15 days on our passing and it paid great dividends," Woody said. "Greene did a great job of scrambling and running."

John McKay, the easygoing Trojan coach, said OSU's passes were very effective.

"I'm not in the business of comparing teams, but as I said before the game, Ohio State is the best team we've played his year," McKay said. "And they can pass."

Hayes was asked if his team deserves to be rated No. 1. "Well, you know I'm a little biased, but yes, today I'd certainly say we were No. 1."

The Buckeyes had led the nation for eight weeks, then slipped to third after its 10-10 tie at Michigan.

Hayes then reiterated that he felt his Buckeyes

could pass on USC. "Greene did a great job. Of course, our receivers (Fred Pagac, Dave Hazel and Brian Baschnagel) made some great catches. It tends to work that way. When you're passing great, the receivers tend to make great catches."

Hayes said Colzie's 56-yard punt return late in the third quarter was the biggest play of the game. "That's the way it's been most of the year. Our defense has been tremendous. They've carried us all the way."

The Buckeye defense let USC quarterback Pat Haden complete 21 of 39 passes for 229 yards, but it stopped him from making the big play.

"We did a good job on defense for as many plays as they had," said Hayes. "And we controlled the ball when we got it."

USC ran 82 plays to 67 for the Buckeyes, but the Buckeyes outgained the Trojans in total yards, 449-406.

Freshman fullback Pete Johnson, who scored three touchdowns on short plunges, had his best day as a Buckeye with 94 yards in 21 carries. Greene followed with 45 and Bruce Elia, who also scored one on a short dive, had 27 yards.

Anthony Davis was USC's leading rusher with 74 yards in 16 tries.

The game was close in the first half, but Ohio State dominated most of the second half, scoring 13 points in the third quarter and 15 in the fourth.

Woody Hayes takes center stage in the Rose Bowl post-game parade after the Buckeyes knocked off Southern Cal.

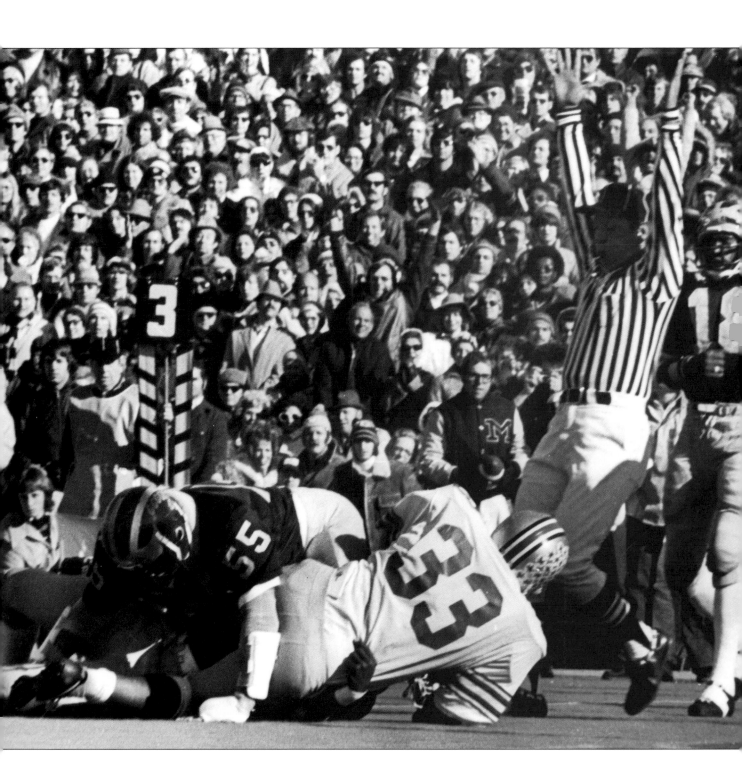

BUCKEYES MAKE BOWL RESERVATIONS AFTER 4TH-QUARTER COMEBACK

Ann Arbor, Mich., Nov. 22, 1975						
Ohio State	7	0	0	14	–	21
Michigan	0	7	0	7	–	14

Woody Hayes called it Ohio State's greatest comeback.

Outplayed for almost three quarters and trailing, 14-7, Ohio State scored twice in the last quarter to overtake Michigan, 21-14, and send the Buckeyes to the Rose Bowl for the fourth straight year.

Fullback Pete Johnson, a 250-pound junior, scored all three OSU touchdowns as the Wolverines lost at home for the first time in six years — a stretch of 41 games.

"Our greatest comeback," Hayes said. "Yes, I'd have to say it was."

Johnson's first score came on a 7-yard pass from Cornelius Greene in the first quarter. His second and third scores were on smashes of 1 and 3 yards in a one-minute span of the final hectic quarter that gave the Buckeyes their 11th straight victory.

Greene brought Ohio State back from the brink of defeat. The senior from Washington moved the Buckeyes 80 yards in 11 plays to tie the score, with

---

The Michigan defense brings Pete Johnson down — but not until the fullback got into the end zone.

Johnson smashing over from a half-foot away on fourth down.

In the drive, Greene fired a 17-yard pass to wingback Brien Baschnagel and followed with two passes in a row to Lenney Willis for 14 and 18 yards.

Tailback Archie Griffin, limited to 46 yards, which ended his 100-yards regular-season rushing streak at 31 games, gained 11 big ones in the drive. Greene then ripped off 12 more to the Michigan 8, and four plays later Johnson scored his 23rd TD of the year with a 1-yard burst off tackle. Tom Klaban booted the extra point that tied the score and that's all Ohio State needed to go to the Rose Bowl.

Hayes revealed in his post-game interview there was never any thought of going for a two-point conversion.

"There was still time to get the ball and we figured we could move it into position for a field goal," Hayes explained.

But the Buckeyes weren't through. They wrapped it up with 2:19 left in the game when Johnson crashed over from 3 yards out after sophomore Ray

Griffin picked off Michigan quarterback Rick Leach's pass on the Wolverine 32 and brought it back to the Michigan 3.

Ohio State fans broke into jubilation and OSU players swarmed over Ray Griffin after his big interception set up the winning score.

"They outplayed us in the first half and the third quarter. Then wasn't it amazing how the game changed," Hayes said.

"This is the greatest comeback I've ever had as coach."

Hayes, who has won 11 Big Ten titles in 25 years at OSU, said Michigan's swarming defense did a good job stopping Griffin's streak.

"But if you know Arch, he'll trade all his records for a victory, like this one," Hayes said.

Michigan, a six-point underdog, played more like the favorite.

The Wolverines came out strong, and although they gave the Buckeyes a 7-0 lead in the first quarter, they came bouncing back in the second.

Leach, a freshman, moved his team 80 yards in 11 plays. The dramatic initial score came when Leach pitched out to Gordon Bell. The fullback then stunned the OSU secondary with an 11-yard pass to wingback Jim Smith, who made a sensational grab in the end zone. Bob Wood converted

Cornelius Greene, with Bill Fleming of ABC-TV, got plenty of attention after being named the Rose Bowl MVP.

to tie the score, 7-7.

Michigan squandered a big opportunity to get on the board when the Wolverines recovered Griffin's fumbled kickoff. But Wood's 37-yard field goal missed left.

Neither team mounted a drive in the third quarter, but the Wolverines definitely had the momentum.

Leach, who hit 7 of 20 passes but had three intercepted, scored the touchdown that put Michigan ahead, 14-7, on a 1-yard smash, which capped a 43-yard Wolverine drive. Wood converted and Michigan was sitting with a seven-point lead.

Up to then Ohio State could not move the ball on the ground or through the air since that first-quarter scoring drive. The Buckeyes had nine possessions and were forced to punt each time because of Michigan's stiff defense.

Then the tide turned. Greene suddenly got his pass protection and went to the air on an 80-yard drive, which pulled the Buckeyes even, 14-14.

Ray Griffin came through with his electrifying pass interception, which set up the winning points.

This was OSU's 11th Big Ten crown and first outright conference title since 1970, but the Buckeyes were co-champs the last three years.

It was Ohio's first victory in Ann Arbor since 1967 and gives Hayes a 4-2-1 edge over Michi-

BUCKEYES VS. MICHIGAN, 1975

gan coach Bo Schembechler, who said no loss is ever easy, "not after that kind of effort we had today."

Everyone but the true partisan Buckeye fans would agree Michigan played a great game and deserved a better fate. But the Wolverines can't be too disappointed. They'll be going to the Orange Bowl to play Oklahoma, which beat Nebraska, 35-10.

Michigan backs Bell and Rob Lytle earned the admiration of the crowd. Bell averaged 5.9 yards

Pete Johnson's touchdown from three yards out with 2:19 left in the game was the difference.

per carry, gaining 124 yards in 21 tries. Lytle had 104 yards in 18 trips.

Michigan had the edge in all statistics except punting, where junior Tom Skladany averaged 44.6 on eight kicks for 357 yards for OSU.

"They outgained us today but in one statistic they didn't finish ahead was the score," said Hayes.

111

Griffin Won More than Two Heisman Trophies – He Won Our Hearts

H e has known for two decades how his epitaph and his obituary will read, and he is quite comfortable with the portrayal.

With many productive years still ahead, some men might consider that lot in life – not to mention death – a bit premature.

Not him.

He knows that no matter what comes later, his legacy is unchangeable.

Chiseled in granite on the tombstone, underneath his name, will be the 11 words that have followed him since college.

And in the obit, first his name, and then that same 11-word phrase encased in commas immediately afterward.

The label did not come from his ancestry. He gave it to himself and no one has yet taken it away or earned the right to share it.

For while there are, no doubt, somewhere in the world, other Archie Griffins, there are, without question, no others who can call themselves by those 11 words:

"The only two-time Heisman Trophy-winner in college football history."

Archie Griffin gave the Buckeyes quite a lift during his incredible four-year stay at Ohio State.

"I expect that sometime, somewhere along the line, somebody is going to win it twice," Archie Griffin says of the award to which he is permanently linked, thanks to his superb junior and senior seasons at Ohio State in 1974 and 1975. "Having that title, 'Two-time Heisman Trophy-winner,' is special to me. It's very, very special to me, but I don't worry about having to share it with someone. I can always say, 'I was the first.'"

Adapting to that possible amendment to his legacy comes as naturally to Griffin, now an associate athletic director at Ohio State, as did his breathtaking cutback runs.

There was then, and is now, simply no ego in the man, even though hero worship rages all around him.

Still the most-requested banquet speaker in the Ohio State athletic department, Griffin accepts the homage paid him by legions of OSU loyalists with the aplomb that once caused his coach, Woody Hayes, to say:

"He's a better young man than he is a football player, and he's the best football player I've ever seen."

No one who watched Griffin lead OSU to four consecutive Rose Bowls from 1972-75 would dispute that latter characterization, for his era lacks only a national championship to make it the undisputed golden age of Ohio State football.

Typically, Griffin would gladly trade one or both of his Heismans for the final No. 1 ranking that eluded OSU his sophomore season because of a 10-10 tie with Michigan, his junior season because of an 18-17 Rose Bowl loss to Southern Cal, and his senior season because of a 23-10 Rose Bowl loss to UCLA.

"We played for it every year," Griffin said. "A win in any one of those three games would have given it to us. That still haunts me. I'd gladly give up those Heismans to have been a national champion, because that would have symbolized how great of a team we were.

"To me, the Heismans also symbolize that, because that success could not happen individually without being part of a great team. I was fortunate to be in the right place at the right time with the right people. I had the opportunity to play with

"He's a better young man than he is a football player, and he's the best football player I've ever seen," Hayes said of Griffin.

guys who made me look good."

Looking good wasn't a description that fit a young Archie Griffin growing up on Columbus' East side.

His football career started modestly as a 9-year-old backup nose guard and offensive lineman in a league full of 12-year-olds.

"My talent didn't get me in that league," Griffin said. "It was a 135-pound weight limit league, and I was too heavy to play with kids my own age."

His friends called him "Tank," and his family called him "Butterball," and both fit the bill until Griffin did something out of desperation.

"Eventually, I just got too heavy to play in that league, and I didn't know of any other leagues in Columbus for young kids to play in before junior high school," he said. "That's when I knew I had to lose the weight."

Lifting makeshift barbells fashioned from a case of beer bottles and a broom handle, running to and from school, wearing plastic bags over his body with the shower steaming hot, Griffin made the load limit for a new team in a new neighborhood on the North side.

Fortuitously, a shortage of fullbacks opened an avenue for him to switch from blocker to ballcarrier, and one three-play sequence that season foreshadowed all the accolades ahead.

Play one: Young Archie blasts off tackle and

storms 50 yards for a touchdown, only to have it nullified by penalty.

Play two: Same call, same result from 5 yards farther away, but again an official's flag brings it back.

Play three: Griffin again, into the line again, touchdown again, this time from 60 yards.

From there it was on to Eastmoor High School and a stellar career as a 160-pound fullback.

"A lot of people told me not to go to Ohio State," Griffin said. "They thought I was too small and that I would get lost in the shuffle there. I listened to that and sort of settled on playing at Northwestern, but I knew if I went to Northwestern, my

parents weren't going to get to see me play.

"What really made the difference, though, was the way Ohio State approached me. They didn't feed me any candy at all. They told me the truth.

"I would always ask coaches, 'When do you think I can play for you? Some would say, 'Right away,' and others would say, 'You'll start in a couple of years.'

"Those weren't the answers I was looking for. I was looking for someone to say, 'If you're good enough, you can play now,' and that's exactly what Coach Hayes told me."

"We could all see that Archie was talented, the question was, 'Would Woody play him?'" said Dave Purdy, the backup quarterback at OSU that season. "Of course, there was no way anyone could have known Archie was going to be as successful as he turned out to be. No one saw that coming."

Certainly not North Carolina, which came to Ohio Stadium for the second game that season.

The Tar Heels had no reason to fear the freshman who had appeared for only one play the week before against Iowa and fumbled a low pitch.

In 27 carries against the Tar Heels, a team that wouldn't lose again that season, Griffin gained 239 yards, an Ohio State single-game rushing record that had stood for 27 years.

Archie Griffin set an NCAA record for the most consecutive 100-yard rushing games with 31.

115

"To this day, of all the games I played in, that's the most exciting one," he said. "I never even expected to play. If I had known the night before I was going to play, I would have been a nervous wreck. As it was, I was really in a daze that whole game. Thank goodness I knew the plays."

Griffin's 900-yard debut season featured a 5.4-yards per carry average and a 30-yard touchdown run against Michigan that made the difference in a 14-11 victory.

That foreshadowed a sophomore year in which he set OSU and Big Ten records with 1,577 rushing yards and made consensus All-American the first of three times.

Griffin also finished fifth in the Heisman Trophy voting that season, three spots behind teammate and runner-up John Hicks.

"In the back of my mind, I thought I had a chance to win the Heisman as a junior, mainly because the four guys who finished ahead of me the year before had graduated," Griffin said. "On the other hand, no one had ever won it twice, so I didn't know what my chances would be."

Breaking both his conference and school marks with a 1,695-yard season didn't hurt.

In 27 carries, Archie Griffin ran for a school-record 239 yards as a freshman against North Carolina.

And breaking Steve Owens' then- NCAA record of 17 straight 100-yard rushing games made Griffin a landslide Heisman winner by more than 1,100 votes over USC's Anthony Davis.

"After winning the Heisman as a junior, it really put the pressure on me for my senior year," Griffin said.

Griffin's output sank to 1,383 yards from 1,695 the year before and his touchdowns declined from 12 as a junior to just four as a senior, creating considerable concern in Columbus that Hayes' love of the Robust T formation on the goal line would hand the Heisman to either California's Chuck Muncie or USC's Ricky Bell.

"A lot of people thought that would cost me the Heisman, but the number of touchdowns I scored never bothered me," Griffin said. "I felt everyone had a role at Ohio State. Throughout my career, whenever I scored, it was from a distance.

"I didn't think that would hurt me as much as I just didn't believe they would give the Heisman to the same person twice."

In retrospect, it's silly to have assumed otherwise, since Griffin smashed the NCAA's career rushing record of 4,715 yards by Cornell's Ed Marinaro in mid-season, finishing with 5,589 yards.

Archie Griffin runs for big yardage against USC in the Rose Bowl. The Buckeyes would lose two of three trips to Pasadena during Griffin's era.

There was also the continually climbing record of 100-yard rushing games, which increased to 31 before Michigan stopped the streak in the regular season's last game.

Ray Griffin made the biggest play in that 21-14 victory, intercepting a Rick Leach pass and returning it to the Wolverines' 3-yard line to set up the winning score with just over one minute remaining.

That night, on the Woody Hayes Show, Hayes walked down the line of players standing before the camera and, tongue firmly in cheek, said: "I'd like you all to meet Ray Griffin's brother, Arch."

A different title, a more permanent title, would come two weeks later when the Downtown Athletic Club summoned Griffin to New York and made him the first and, so far, the only, two-time winner of collegiate football's most coveted award.

The vote wasn't close, with Muncie in second, more than 1,000 votes behind.

"It seems to be a part of my name now," Griffin said. "Whenever I'm mentioned, it's always, 'Two-time Heisman Trophy-winner.' It's become a part of my life. It's something I never thought would happen to me, so I consider it a bonus. I cherish it very much."

The Sooners used three different quarterbacks during their visit to Columbus and ran off with a victory.

SOONERS STUN BUCKEYES
ON LATE FIELD GOAL

Columbus, Sept. 24, 1977						
Oklahoma	17	3	0	9	–	29
Ohio State	0	14	14	0	–	28

Uwe von Schamann kicked a 41-yard field goal with three seconds left, giving Oklahoma a dramatic 29-28 victory over Ohio State before 88,113.

The kick by von Schamann climaxed an uphill struggle for the Sooners, who shot out to a 20-0 lead in the second quarter over the stunned Buckeyes, and then battled back with a touchdown and field goal in the final 1:29 of the game to win.

"I knew it was going through when I kicked it, and the screaming crowd really didn't bother me," said von Schamann.

Elvis Peacock scored on a 1-yard sweep to pull Oklahoma within two points of the Buckeyes, 28-26. The Sooners went for two, but Peacock was stopped short by OSU safety Mike Guess on a sweep.

The third largest crowd in Ohio State history gave a roar of approval and sensed victory was at hand, but the Sooners were not through.

The Buckeyes were prepared for the on-side kick, but von Schamann's squib kick was recovered by Mike Babb after it first touched an OSU player.

Dean Blevins, one of three quarterbacks used by the Sooners, hit Steve Rhodes with an 18-yard pass, and three running plays put the Sooners on the OSU 26 with 26 seconds to play.

After Oklahoma had called timeout and the teams lined up for von Schamann's field-goal attempt, the Buckeyes called timeout with six seconds left. Here Schamann knelt down by himself, head bowed, and tried to collect his thoughts.

The crowd shouted, "Block that kick!" as von

Uwe von Schamann celebrates his winning 41-yard field goal, which came with three seconds left in the game.

Schamann got up. "I knew what the crowd was trying to do," he said. "I didn't want it to bother me. I put everything out of my mind."

Von Schamann, who kicked field goals of 23 and 33 yards and booted two PAT's, said the pressure didn't bother him.

"I knew I had the wind and that helped," said the soccer-style kicker who was born in West Berlin and came to Forth Worth, Texas, with his parents when he was 14.

"The snap was perfect and I hit it right on the nose," von Schamann said.

The big field goal enabled the Sooners to win a game they felt they had lost because of numerous mistakes after starting quarterback Thomas Lott went out with an injured left knee early in the contest.

After scoring two quick touchdowns and a field goal, Oklahoma had the situation in control after von Schamann booted a 33-yard field goal early in the second for a 20-0 lead.

But the momentum suddenly went to the Buckeyes. Their defense came alive and offense perked up with the home team scoring twice — Ron Springs scampering 31 yards and quarterback Rod Gerald dashing 19 to put them within six points, 20-14.

BUCKEYES BEATEN; WOODY STRIKES FOE

Jacksonville, Fla., Dec. 28, 1978						
Ohio State	0	9	0	6	–	15
Clemson	0	10	7	0	–	17

Clemson's tenacious Tigers won their first post-season football game in 19 years when they outmuscled Ohio State, 17-15, in the Gator Bowl before 72,011.

Middle guard Charlie Bauman intercepted Art Schlichter to snuff out Ohio State's last chance to win the game.

Bauman's catch sparked a near riot after he picked off Schlichter's pass on the Clemson 18 with 1:59 left in the game. Bauman was tackled by

120

Schlichter as the two fell out of bounds near the Ohio State bench.

Bauman appeared to say a few words to the Ohio State bench and Buckeye coach Woody Hayes, standing beside the Clemson middle guard, delivered a punch with his right fist just under the chin.

Tempers flared and both teams poured out on the field as officials and coaches tried to restrain the players.

Hayes had to be pulled away by assistant coach George Hill when Hayes went out to protest an unsportsmanlike penalty. Hayes jawed at the officials, who promptly gave Ohio State another 15-yard penalty for unsportsmanlike conduct.

It was another disgraceful performance by Hayes, who has had his share of outbursts in 28 years at Ohio State, and it blackened an already bad image before a national television audience.

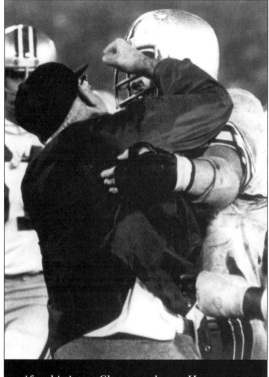

After hitting a Clemson player, Hayes turned on one of his own, punching a Buckeye in the facemask.

It was a big victory from Clemson coach Danny Ford, 30, who made his first start as a head coach a successful one.

"Boy, they were all great ... Steve Fuller, Marvin Sims, Warren Ratchford, but Bauman's interception was it," said Ford.

Hayes did not talk to the press after the wild ending. Instead, he sent Hill, his defensive coordinator, to speak to the media outside of the Buckeye locker room.

Hill was asked what happened on the field when Hayes had his outburst and was assessed two unsportsmanlike penalties. "I didn't see what happened and for me to comment would not be proper," he said. "I was there, but still couldn't see and I can't comment on something I didn't see."

Schlichter, who was voted the outstanding Ohio State player of the game after completing 15 of 21 passes for 205 yards, was praised by Hill. "Art threw as well tonight as in any game this year," Hill said.

"Our team played hard, but made too many mistakes to win. Our defense played extremely hard and Tom Cousineau (All-America linebacker from Lakewood St. Edward) played his guts out. He is a great, great, great football player."

After squandering two chances to get on the scoreboard with field goals in the first quarter, the Buckeyes took a 3-0 lead on a 27-yard field goal by Bob Atha to cap an eight-play, 72-yard drive early in the second quarter.

Ohio State moved to the Clemson 2 and the 21 in the first quarter but did not score. On both tries, the

Buckeyes faced fourth-and-short yardage situations and elected to go for the first down, only to be stopped.

On their first possession the Buckeyes drove to the Clemson 2, where fullback Paul Campbell hit the middle of the line and was stopped. It was an impressive march with Springs, Campbell and Schlichter running the ball.

Campbell came up short again when the Buckeyes advanced to the 21 and needed one yard.

The Buckeyes broke the spell on the 72-yard drive to the field goal.

A pass from Schlichter to Doug Donley for 34 yards and another for 6 to Campbell were the big gainers. Rod Gerald clicked on an eight-yard reverse to help the advance, but Clemson's defense braced and Atha was summoned for his field goal.

Clemson countered with its best drive, moving 80 yards to take a 7-3 lead as Fuller, the quarterback, scored from the 4-yard line. His score came with 5:03 remaining and closed the gap to 7-3 after Oded Ariri booted the extra point.

On the next kickoff, Ohio State took command again as Schlichter showed his fancy aerial work by completing 3 of 3 for 54 yards.

The dazzler in this drive was a 34-yard pass to 6-8 Ron Barwig, who snagged the ball and carried to the Clemson 9. On the next play, Schlichter gained five to the 4, and on the next play the rook-

A dejected Tom Cousineau, the OSU linebacker, after an emotional loss.

ie smashed over the left side for the score. The extra point by Vlade Jankiewski was blocked, leaving the Buckeyes on top, 9-7.

Clemson went to the air in the remaining 1:21 before the half. With Fuller firing strikes of 17, 20, 28 and 10 yards, the Tigers quickly moved to the OSU 30. However, the Buckeyes held and Ariri was summoned for another field-goal attempt. He split the uprights from 47 yards with five seconds left to give Clemson the lead again, 10-9.

Clemson came out for the second half breathing fire. The Tigers stopped Ohio State the first two times the Buckeyes had the ball, and then the ACC champs ran right at OSU as they marched 84 yards to take a 17-9 lead.

The running of Fuller, Sims and Warren Ratchford made it look easy for the Tigers as they ripped huge holes in the OSU defense to march to the 1.

Twice Ohio State braced to stop Ratchford as he tried to get into the end zone. Once he was stopped by Cousineau, who slammed Ratchford to the ground with a jarring tackle.

On third-and-1, tailback Cliff Austin hurtled over the center of the line for the touchdown and Ariri kicked his second extra point to give the Tigers a seven-point lead. The Buckeyes could not generate any sustained movement as the Clemson defense bottled them up.

Firing of Hayes End of an Era

Woody Hayes was fired yesterday and the search for a successor begins Tuesday when a committee will be formed to find a new Ohio State football coach.

Hayes, 65, and for 28 years the head coach of the Buckeyes, was fired for his unsportsmanlike conduct in the Gator Bowl, where he punched a Clemson player during the Buckeyes' 17-15 loss.

The announcement was made at a 10 a.m. press conference by Hugh Hindman, the OSU athletic director, who issued the following statement:

"Woody Hayes has been relieved of his duties as head coach of Ohio State University. This decision has the full support of the president of the university, Harold Enarson."

Hindman said firing Hayes was an "extremely difficult decision" for him because he played for Hayes one year at Miami of Ohio and was his line coach at Ohio State for seven years.

During a news conference last night at the Pittsburgh airport, where the charter plane carrying Ohio State officials was forced to land because of heavy fog in Columbus, Enarson said he supported Hindman's decision.

Hayes erupted on the sidelines late in the game, punching two of his players and hitting Clemson middle guard Charlie Bauman three times in full view of a national TV audience.

Hindman said he went to the OSU locker room after the game and offered Hayes the opportunity to resign.

"Hayes told me, 'I'm not going to resign. It would be too easy for you. You better go ahead and fire me,'" Hindman said.

Enarson was asked how embarrassing this was to OSU.

"It's difficult to say. There is a certain amount of anguish I feel. I comfort myself with a keen awareness that football has totally suffered," Enarson said.

"I did not see the melee on the field as I was heading for the buses back to our lodge. And it wasn't until after 2 a.m. that Hugh came over and told me of the situation.

"I, along with many people, feel great sadness for a coach with such an illustrious record for a quarter of a century to leave the business in this tragic fashion.

"There's not a university or athletic conference in the country that would permit a coach to physically assault a college athlete."

Hindman says there is not a timetable to find a successor, "but it must be done as quickly as possible."

Will Hayes be offered some other university post?

"We haven't discussed this," Enarson said.

123

Charismatic Woody Hayes Was Ohio State Football for 28 Years

I t is the first 80-degree day of an otherwise obstinate Ohio spring, a day to think about anything but football or a coach 20 years removed from the field and gone to that sideline in the sky a full decade ago. But while men die and the memories of them fade, legends never leave, nor does their effect.

From quarterbacks to politicians, Woody Hayes could teach the game of football like no other. At left, he talks strategy with QB Dave Leggett. Below, he poses with Vice President Richard Nixon.

That is why the Ohio State University Scarlet Golf Course is dotted this day with thick-necked former players whose backswings need a little work, but whose follow-throughs – in life, if not on the links – need no improvement.

All of them undoubtedly have other things to do, if not better things to do.

But all of them have forsaken the

Critics often complained of the way Woody Hayes berated officials during the game.

So that's what the collection of former Buckeyes from the 1950's, '60's and '70's in the 21st Woody Hayes Celebrity Golf Classic are doing — paying homage to the coach whose admonitions about conduct and character have outlived the Xs and Os he diagrammed.

More than $1 million has been raised by this event since its inception, allowing untold patients at Children's Hospital in Columbus and its Center for Child Abuse Prevention to benefit from a man whose existence remains a paradox to all but those who knew him best.

That would greatly please The Old Man, as his players and peers affectionately came to call him, because then he would know they heeded his call to "help young people as someone helped you when you were young. Invest in the future."

That was the theme of countless Hayes speeches, most of them gratis, after his firing from Ohio State in 1978.

The 238-72-10 record that made him the fourth-winningest coach in history when he bowed out never came up much, nor did his 205-61-10 mark at OSU that featured national championships in 1954, 1961 and 1968, 13 Big Ten titles and seven Rose Bowl appearances.

"I don't live in the past," Hayes said shortly before his death in March of 1987. "I'm a student

demands of their business and the duties of their personal lives because, no matter how sunny a day it is, none of them can escape the shadow of one man's influence.

"You can never pay back, but you can always pay forward," Woody Hayes used to tell them.

of the past, and I try to learn from the past, although some people will say, 'You haven't done a very good job of it.' But for me to live in the past? Hell, no."

This explains why Hayes expressed only grudging regret for the incident that brought an unfortunate end to his career in 1978, a frustrated punch of Clemson linebacker Charlie Bauman after his interception sealed OSU's 17-15 Gator Bowl defeat.

Hayes' stance on that never wavered much from the first speech he gave three weeks after his termination.

"I don't apologize for anything," he said. "When I make a mistake, I take the blame for it and go on from there. I just despise to lose, and that has taken a man of mediocre ability and made a pretty good coach out of him."

Good enough to produce 58 All-Americans and three Heisman Trophy winners, all of whom Hayes was less likely to boast about than he was the three players who emerged from OSU's medical school with the highest grade-point average in the class during one three-year stretch of the 1960's.

"Next to my father, he was the greatest man I ever knew," said Rod Gerald, a quarterback who played for Hayes from 1975-78, and who the old coach badgered to turn his life around from drug abuse.

Shortly after Hayes' death, Gerald kicked his

Woody Hayes and Paul (Bear) Bryant (right) will forever be associated with college football success.

drug habit, obtained his degree and settled into a happy marriage with children.

That was the side of Hayes others seldom saw. The side, in fact, he worked to keep others from seeing.

All of it, the warts and the wonder, made him the most captivating, charismatic and confounding figure in the history of Ohio State's football, if not the entire university.

"You don't describe Woody Hayes in one word, one sentence or one paragraph," Hayes' 22-year assistant, Esco Sarkkinen, once said. "You describe him with chapter after chapter."

That's been done by a collection of authors, and still the mysteries beg to be reconciled.

The coach known for tearing his cap, smashing his wristwatch and stomping his glasses in fits of rage, was also prone to tears at the slightest sentimentality.

The coach so headstrong he often left the apologies for his embarrassing tantrums to administrative underlings, was also so impressionable he took to walking the two miles to his office rather than drive his car and exacerbate America's energy crisis.

The coach so intolerant of technical errors and turnovers that the slightest such error could set off a seismic eruption, was also so forgiving that when

127

a doctor confessed to post-surgical complications being the result of a sponge mistakenly being sewn inside Hayes' abdominal cavity, The Old Man simply smiled and said: "Gee, that's funny. In 28 years of coaching, I never made a mistake."

To many, he did not, and to others, he made legions, but regardless of the view, there was no disputing the degree of Hayes' commitment to Ohio State.

"Whether it was Bo Schembechler, Bill Mallory, Lou Holtz, Dave McClain, Earle Bruce, Rudy Hubbard or whoever, we all coached the same when we became head coaches," said Holtz, OSU's defensive backfield coach in 1968.

Nowhere was Hayes' commitment more complete than in his insatiable desire to defeat Michigan.

Woody Hayes and Penn State's Joe Paterno share a laugh before a game in 1975. The Buckeyes won, 17-9.

The Wolverines had won the previous four Big Ten championships and hadn't lost to Ohio State in seven years when Hayes was hired in 1951.

Over the next 18 years, Michigan would manage only a solitary conference title to OSU's five and the Buckeyes would dominate the series, winning 12 and losing six.

Things changed in 1969 when Schembechler took over at Michigan.

The rivalry grew exponentially in spirit and in stature during he and Hayes' 10 chess matches, a decade in which the two teams so dominated the conference it became known as The Big Two and the Little Eight.

Schembechler won the head-to-head battle with the man he assisted at OSU from 1959-63 by a 5-4-1 margin, but each team wound up going to five Rose Bowls over that span.

Nothing stirred the passions in Hayes more passionately than the annual border war with "that team up north."

He would exercise every edge possible in search of victory, sometimes practicing one day a week for Michigan amid preparations for the other teams on his schedule, and occasionally all week for the Wolverines when a weak opponent was next in line.

Hayes' favorite motivational tactic, however, was to bring past players to practice during game week and have them speak about the game's significance.

"I'll never forget, one year I was playing in the CFL and I got a call that Coach Hayes needed me to come in and do something special the week of the Michigan game," said Jim Stillwagon, the middle guard on OSU's 1968 national champions and the first double winner of the Outland and Lombardi trophies. "So I get there and he says to me, 'You have to tell them what it's like to play in the big game. You have to tell them what it means.'

"So, I get out there after practice and I start in with whatever it was I said and all the sudden Woody just goes into this frenzy.

"'Yeah, but I mean, tell 'em how it really bleep-

ing was.' BAM. He hits me right in the stomach. 'Tell em it's like war.' BAM. He hits me again. 'You gotta kill those sons of bitches.' BAM.

"I'm getting the snot beat out of me. It's like he's hitting a heavy bag. BAM. 'Now, you tell 'em, Jim.' And I'm thinking to myself, 'How did I get into this?'

"But you know what? Every guy who was there told me later, 'That was a great speech you gave.' "

It must have been.

The next day, Ohio State held twice on its 1-yard line to capture that 1972 game, 14-11, and start a four-year streak of Rose Bowl appearances that denied Michigan a single trip to Pasadena despite a 38-4-3 overall record during that period.

Schembechler evened the score by winning three straight from Hayes at the end of their Ten Year War, but the victories were bittersweet in bringing a conclusion to their competition.

"The rivalry lost a little something without him," Schembechler said. "It had to. The man had the greatest impact on this conference since its incep-

Bo Schembechler (left) and Woody Hayes met 10 times with Schembechler finishing 5-4-1 against his mentor.

tion. He was one of the greatest coaches who ever lived."

Certainly, there has been no greater coach at OSU. For proof, consider this:

■ The Buckeyes had four unbeaten seasons in 60 years of football before Hayes' arrival.

■ They experienced four more during his 28 seasons.

■ They have experienced none since his departure.

"I can't imagine that there will ever be another Woody Hayes," two-time Heisman Trophy winner Archie Griffin said. "It would be kind of hard to be a Woody Hayes in these times.

"I say that because people have changed and attitudes have changed. The way Coach Hayes showed he cared about you was to get on you for your mistakes, but then build you up afterward. That's what players loved about him.

OHIO STATE DEFEATS MICHIGAN

C oach Earle Bruce, raspy-voiced and smiling broadly, summed up Ohio State's 18-15 victory over Michigan by saying the unbeaten Buckeyes are going to the Rose Bowl in the right way.

"It was a great effort by the Buckeyes," he said. "It's been a great season. Our young men have responded to everything we've demanded. Before the game I told the players to go out and play like we have in the last 10."

Ohio State beat Michigan for the first time since 1975 and ended a 15-quarter touchdown drought against the Wolverines. The game was played before an NCAA regular-season record crowd of 106,255

Ann Arbor, Mich., Nov. 17, 1979					
Ohio State	0	6	6	6	– 18
Michigan	0	7	8	0	– 15

Quarterback Art Schlichter tries to escape Ann Arbor with the game ball after the Buckeyes won, 18-15.

130

— and the largest ever in Michigan Stadium.

With the victory goes the Big Ten championship, the Buckeyes' 22nd overall and ninth outright.

The Buckeyes scored two second-half touchdowns and had control of the game after intermission, although Michigan had a 15-12 lead at one point.

The Buckeyes, getting two field goals from Vlade Janakievski (23 and 25 yards) in the first half and four excellent punts from Tom Orosz (for a 40.5 average),

Art Schlichter gets a victory ride from Ohio State fans who made the trip north to Ann Arbor.

dominated this phase as Michigan came up woefully short.

The OSU defense won the game when linebacker Jim Laughlin, senior defensive co-captain from Lyndhurst, blocked Bryan Virgil's punt early in the fourth quarter. Todd Bell picked up the ball on the 15-yard line and went in for an easy score — his second of the season. He did the same thing at Illinois.

That was the game for all practical reasons, because the Buckeye defense was playing so well. The defense limited Michigan to 68 yards on the ground.

Yesterday was the fourth time this season that Michigan has had a blocked punt turned into a score.

"We rushed 10 men on that punt," Bruce said. "Earlier, they tried to throw a pass on us and we had been set to rush 10 men but dropped two back."

Laughlin said he had a clear shot at Virgil. "With

our 10-man rush, we send a couple up the middle, so I had a free lane on the right side," Laughlin explained.

"This is the greatest feeling in the world — winning today. I'm so proud to be a member of this Ohio State team, which has done a great job of responding."

Quarterback Art Schlichter had a super day, even though he said the wind bothered him. The 6-3, 200-pound sophomore hit Chuck Hunter with a 19-yard scoring pass late in the third period that put OSU ahead, 12-7.

"I thought my passes were close, but a couple were off. The wind bothered me. At times it picked up and at others it was calm."

Schlichter completed 12 of 22 for 196 yards and had one intercepted. It was the fifth time he had been intercepted this season, compared to 21 in his freshman season. He ran the option 15 times for just 27 yards.

Schlichter's aerial work led to OSU's second field goal. He fired passes to Doug Donley for 26 and 18 yards, hit freshman Gary Williams on a 22-yarder, and Jim Gayle on one for 6. The 80-yard drive stalled on the U-M 8, where Janakievski kicked a 25-yard field goal.

What did the victory mean to Schlichter?

"My main goal was for us to go unbeaten," he said. "It's the greatest feeling in the world."

Michigan coach Bo Schembechler surprised the crowd and a national TV audience when he started freshman Rick Hewlett at quarterback.

"I wanted to run the option to improve our ground game," Bo said. "We were going to alternate quarterbacks."

Was Ohio State prepared to face Hewlett?

"We didn't know who was going to start," Bruce said. "We didn't know anything about Hewlett. We figured (John) Wangler would start. But Hewlett backfired, and then they went to Wangler."

Wangler, a senior, burned OSU twice by hitting

Ohio State kicker Vlade Janakievski (13) nailed two field goals (23 and 25 yards) in the first half.

two long bombs to receiver Anthony Carter.

One was a 59-yard TD pass in the second quarter, the other a 66-yard play that Carter took to the Ohio 19. Seven plays later Roosevelt Smith scored from the 1. Smith then smashed up the middle to give Michigan two points on the conversion attempt, and the Wolverines took a 15-12 lead.

Wangler finished with 133 yards, hitting 4 of 9 with one interception. Hewlett was 1 of 4 with one interception. Hewlett also ran for 20 yards.

Tailback Butch Woolfolk led the Michigan ground attack with 68 yards.

Gayle, who went in for Calvin Murray when Murray suffered a hip bruise, was OSU's surprise runner with 72 yards in nine carries for an 8.0 average. Paul Campbell had 39, Tim Spencer 37, Rick Volley 23 and Murray 38.

Bruce said he plans to give the squad some time off before beginning preparations for the Rose Bowl.

Did he expect Ohio State to go 11-0?

"Most certainly," he answered with a wide grin. "I'm a positive guy."

Michigan, which finished the regular season 8-3, has accepted an invitation to play in the Gator Bowl against North Carolina.

ROSES ARE WHITE'S, BUCKEYES ARE BLUE

Ohio State's Gary Williams keeps one step ahead of Southern Cal's Kenny Moore (43).

O hio State fullback Paul Campbell best summarized how the Buckeyes felt about Southern Cal tailback Charles White.

"He's a great back, period," Campbell said. "He's like the Buckeyes. He doesn't quit."

White was a one-man destruction team as he led favored Southern Cal to a come-from-behind, 17-16 victory over the gutty Buckeyes in the Rose Bowl.

It was witnessed by 105,526 and a national television audience.

White rushed for 247 yards in 39 carries. He scored the touchdown that tied the game on a 1-yard smash with 1:32 to play.

Pasadena, Calif., Jan. 1, 1980					
USC	3	7	0	7	– 17
Ohio State	0	10	3	3	– 16

Then Eric Hipp kicked the extra point for the 17th Rose Bowl victory in the Trojans' history, their second in a row, and handed the Big Ten its sixth straight Rose Bowl setback and 10th in the last 11 years.

Trailing 16-10, USC started the winning drive with 5:21 left to play. The drive covered 83 yards. White accounted for 65 of those yards with runs of 32 and 33 yards. He was unstoppable, and when he smashed over to cap the drive, Trojan partisans went wild, shouting, "We're No. 1!"

Whether they will be voted first will be determined when the final Associated Press poll is announced later this week.

Coach John Robinson of USC said his team deserves consideration for No. 1.

"We beat the No. 1 team in dramatic fashion," Robinson said. "Alabama deserves consideration, but we have not lost a game and we've tied Stanford. I've got a good idea on who I'm voting for."

Robinson, who just signed a new, five-year contract to coach at USC, called it "one of the greatest football games," and he praised the Buckeyes as "tremendous competitors."

"Ohio State played a great game. USC played a great game. There were a lot of mistakes, coaching mistakes, but it was still a great game."

White, the Heisman Trophy winner, with exceptional acceleration and ability to get extra yards, was everything he was advertised to be.

"Charlie White is the best football player I have ever seen," Robinson said in the locker room after the game.

"If there is any doubt about how good he is, go back through the fourth quarter. his dominance was incredible. He is the finest athlete and the greatest competitor."

Coach Earle Bruce, who led OSU to an 11-0 record going into the game, thought the Buckeyes gave a very good account of themselves.

"It was an excellent football game for us, except for SC's last down," said Bruce. "That was a great drive and they simply out-executed us. But, on the whole, I was very pleased with our defensive play. USC is a very explosive team. They are everything they said they were."

Linebacker Jim Laughlin, senior co-captain from Lyndhurst and Brush High, said the Trojans used two basic plays on the last drive that won the game.

"The pitch and lead sweep with isolation," Laughlin said. "White is so good. He found the hole and burst through. We thought we could stop him.

"He has the ability to find a seam in a defense, no matter how small, and get through, and he has great second effort."

Douglas Donley (47) is the first to greet Gary Williams after Ohio State's second-quarter touchdown.

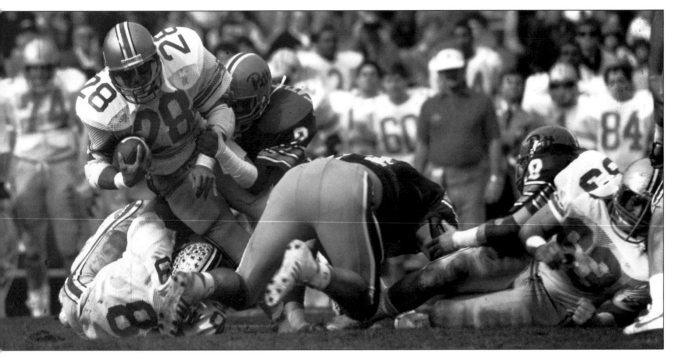

With the victory over Pitt, the Buckeyes evened their all-time bowl record to 9-9.

OHIO STATE BOMBS PITT IN FIESTA

Tempe, Ariz., Jan. 2, 1984						
Ohio State	7	7	0	14	–	28
Pittsburgh	0	7	0	16	–	23

T had Jemison's last game for Ohio State will be a memorable one.

After sitting on the bench as an understudy to Gary Williams for three years, Jemison finally received his moment of glory when he caught a 39-yard touchdown pass with 39 seconds left from quarterback

Mike Tomczak that gave the Buckeyes a 28-23 victory over Pitt in the Fiesta Bowl before 66,484 in Sun Devil Stadium.

Jemison, a 6-2, 195-pound senior from Cincinnati, said it was frustrating to sit and wait. He was patient, however, and it paid off. This season he became the starting split end, but he still played in the shadow of tight end John Frank and tailback Keith Byars, who were the principal pass catchers.

Going into this post-season game, Jemison had caught only two touchdown passes, against Wisconsin and Indiana.

Given the chance, he made up his mind that the Fiesta Bowl would be his chance to shine. Jemison was the key in OSU's victory — the third straight in postseason play — by making eight catches for 131 yards. His last one will stay with him for a long time.

"I really feel good the way the game finished," Jemison said. "It was a fine way to end my career."

On the touchdown pass that won the game, Jemison said, "They double covered the tight end (Frank) and the flanker (Cedric Anderson) and I was open."

Jemison's eight catches tied the Fiesta Bowl record set by John Jefferson of Arizona State in 1975. Pitt's Bill Wallace also tied the mark with eight catches for 97 yards.

Before the Tomczak-Jemison winning play, it looked as if the Buckeyes were headed for defeat. The see-saw thriller came to the last quarter and it looked as if the Panthers had staked their claim to victory when Snuffy Everett kicked a 37-yard field goal that lifted the underdog Panthers into a 23-21 lead.

What further darkened the Buckeyes' chances came on the next kickoff when John Wooldridge caught the ball at the 10 and his knee touched the ground.

But the Buckeyes were undaunted as they went to work with 2:30 left. Tomczak, who completed 15 of 32 for 226 yards for the day, moved the team to the Pitt 39. With 39 seconds remaining, he rolled to his right and saw Jemison speeding for the end zone. The ball was perfectly timed and caught. Rich Spangler kicked the extra point and the Buckeyes had evened their all-time bowl record at 9-9.

The Buckeyes' offense passed for 226 yards against Pitt.

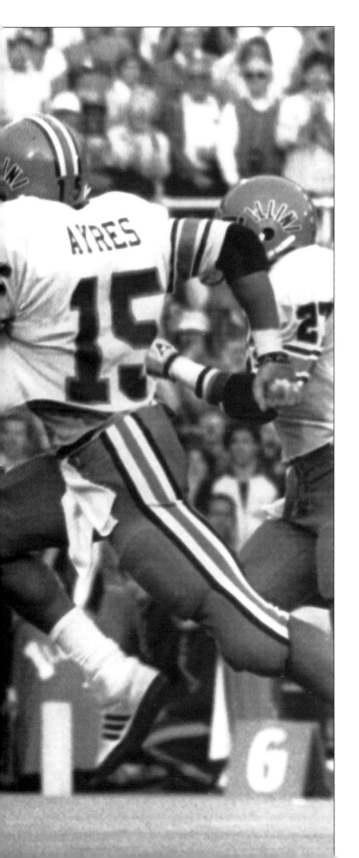

BUCKEYES' RALLY TOPS ILLINI

K eith Byars rewrote a lot of the Ohio State record book, leading the Buckeyes to a 45-38 triumph over Illinois. The Buckeyes rallied from a 24-point deficit before 89,937, the second-largest crowd in Ohio Stadium history.

The 6-2, 233-pound Byars rambled for 274 yards in 39 carries and scored five touchdowns on the eve of his 21st birthday. His 274 yards erased Archie Griffin's single-game rushing record of 246, which came against Iowa in 1973. The five touchdowns Byars scored tied Pete Johnson's school record.

Another benefit of Byars' effort was that it enabled the Buckeyes to move back into a first-place tie for

Columbus, Oct. 13, 1984						
Illinois	17	7	11	3	–	38
Ohio State	0	21	14	10	–	45

Keith Byars' 67-yard touchdown run in the third quarter proved that great backs only need one shoe.

the Big Ten lead with Purdue, Michigan and Iowa.

"If there is a more spectacular back in college football, I don't know where he is," said Earle Bruce. "I watch him every day and know how hard he works. He's truly a great, great tailback."

The most spectacular of Byars' touchdown runs was a 67-yard sprint in the third quarter.

Byars circled right end, cut back inside, lost his left shoe at the Illini 35, but never slowed down in outrunning Illinois' secondary.

"I just felt my shoe slipping off, but there was no way I was going to go back and get it," said Byars. "I didn't know I was close to breaking Archie Griffin's record until I saw it on the scoreboard.

"Running the ball is a two-way street at Ohio State. The linemen block for me and I run for them. I wasn't at all tired in the fourth quarter, but I am now.

"When we were behind, 24-0, I told myself that the season was on the line and now was the time for me to do it."

By rushing for 274 yards, Byars pushed his season total to 1,076. Griffin's season-rushing record of 1,695, which he set in 1974, is within Byars' reach, in this, Byars' junior season.

"Keith Byars did it all," said Mike White, the Illini coach. "He is so sudden, so versatile and has everything a good back needs. He is equal to any college back I have been around."

Keith Byars climbs the mountain for one of his five touchdowns, tying Pete Johnson's school record for TDs in a game.

Illinois appeared as though it was going to drive OSU right into the ground until Byars ignited the Buckeyes' offense.

Byars launched OSU's comeback in the second quarter by capping a 91-yard, 10-play drive with a 16-yard touchdown run.

Quarterback Mike Tomczak connected with freshman wide receiver Cris Carter on a 30-yard play to trim the Illini lead to 24-14. Byars leaped into the end zone on a 4-yard run to enable OSU to keep its comeback moving right before halftime.

There was to be no slowing down by Byars in the second half. He gained all 26 yards in OSU's fourth scoring drive that followed the Buckeyes recovery of Ray Wilson's fumble of the opening kickoff of the second half. Byars' 1-yard plunge put OSU ahead, 27-24, and Rich Spangler, perfect on all his kicks, booted the extra point.

Chris White then kicked a 46-yard field goal for the Illini.

Wilson grabbed a 9-yard strike from Jack Trudeau to tie the game at 35-35 with 1:09 remaining in the third quarter.

Byars and Wooldridge alternated carrying the ball on OSU's last scoring drive, which began at its 20.

After Illinois stalled the Buckeyes' march at its 3-yard line for one play, Byars took a pitch around left end and darted into the end zone for the game-winning TD.

Tomczak Passes as Leader

Mike Tomczak was 16-of-26 passing for 236 yards and one TD against Illinois.

Thirteen seconds into the second quarter and even the hard-core Ohio State fans were paralyzed by thoughts of a humiliating defeat.

Quarterback Jack Trudeau and Illinois' Fighting Illini were putting points on the scoreboard almost at will. Trudeau's strike to tight end Cap Boso with 14:47 left in the half gave the Illini a 24-0 lead, and probably made the Ohio State homecoming queen and her court give serious thought to making their way to the dance early.

Surely Coach Earle Bruce wasn't aware of it at the time, but the Buckeyes were caught in the grip of Woody Hayes' revenge.

Why pass the football, as long as there's a running back standing. And, of course, the Buckeyes are blessed with Keith Byars, the nation's best running back.

But it was not until the second time Ohio State had the ball in the second quarter that Bruce seemed to remember that he had a pretty good quarterback, too.

Mike Tomczak completed four straight passes, leading the Buckeyes to their first touchdown with 4:13 left in the half. And predictably, Byars' awesome charges at the Illini defense were even more meaningful.

"We are a running team," Bruce explained afterward, "and we use the pass when we have to."

Perhaps, but it was the passing of Tomczak, starting his fourth game since returning from a near career-ending fracture of his right leg, who made it all possible.

"That's the kind of help we expect from our passing game," Bruce said of Tomczak's 16 completions of 26 passes for 236 yards and one touchdown. "We won it and we won it with Keith Byars and Mike Tomczak and Cris Carter."

GREATEST MOMENTS IN OHIO STATE FOOTBALL HISTORY

BUCKEYES WHIP U-M, WIN ROSE PRIZE

Columbus, Nov. 17, 1984					
Michigan	0	3	3	0 –	6
Ohio State	7	0	14	0 –	21

Woody Hayes had to be smiling to himself in the press box.

Ohio State had just returned to the kind of old-fashioned, power football he made famous.

The result was a 21-6 victory over Michigan as the Buckeyes earned their first trip to the Rose Bowl in five years.

A record crowd of 90,286 saw Coach Earle Bruce scrap the Buckeyes' three-wideout formation for the Power-I in the second half.

Keith Byars' talent did the rest. Byars, who scored all three OSU TDs, smashed over the goal line twice on short runs in the fourth quarter.

Byars, however, came up short in his pursuit of Archie Griffin's Big Ten single-season rushing record of 1,695 yards. He needed 142 yards to break it. He finished with 113 in 28 carries.

"This is something that I've dreamed about all my life," Byars said. "Beating Michigan, winning the Big Ten championship and getting to play Southern Cal in the Rose Bowl."

Until the fourth quarter, OSU's offense behaved as though it didn't care where it spent its holidays. Michigan's defensive quickness was preventing Byars from turning upfield on numerous option plays.

The Wolverines limited him to 45 yards in 13 carries in the first half and tackled him for 15 yards in losses.

OSU was clinging to a 7-6 lead in the fourth quarter before it started its punishing assault.

Michigan almost deflated the Buckeyes' hopes in the third quarter. Sophomore Chris Zurbrugg moved the Wolverines from their 10-yard line to the OSU 19, where Michigan was hit with an illegal procedure penalty in a second-and-4 situation that sent Michigan coach Bo Schembechler into a tirade.

The penalty moved the ball back to the OSU 24 and Michigan ended up settling for a 45-yard field goal by Bob Bergeron and a 7-6 deficit.

"I thought we had a great shot to win, and we should have won it," said Schembechler, who finished with his worst record in 16 years at Michigan at 6-5.

"Ohio State is a good team, but I concede nothing to them. We tossed away too many good opportunities and the officials did not help. But you can

Ohio State's Keith Byars leaps over Michigan defenders and into the end zone giving the Buckeyes a 13-6 lead.

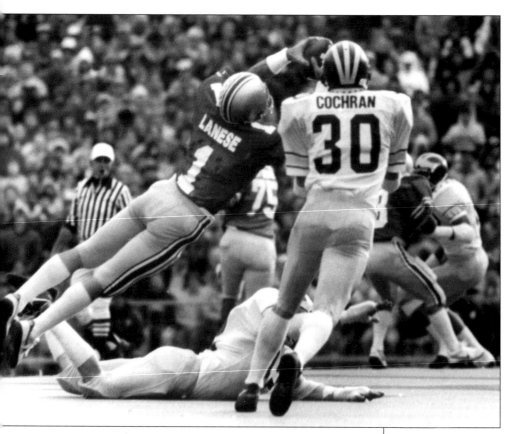

Mike Lanese dives to catch a Mike Tomczak pass during the Buckeyes' 21-6 victory over Michigan.

expect that in this league."

Michigan could have changed the flow of the game if Bergeron had made a 34-yard field-goal try late in the third quarter. But his attempt sailed to the right.

Ohio State's effort to harness its offensive energies following Bergeron's miss failed. The Buckeyes ran five plays before being forced to punt.

The Wolverines shortly returned the favor. Ohio State took over at its 45.

Mike Tomczak was sacked on the first play by tackle Kevin Brooks for a 4-yard loss. Byars was stopped after a 2-yard gain and OSU faced a third down needing 12 yards for a first down.

Flanker Mike Lanese caught a 17-yard pass to keep the drive alive. Lanese's catch moved the ball to the Michigan 43.

Bruce decided to go back to power football and Ohio State steadily moved the ball and scored when Byars dove over from the 2.

Byars' TD increased Ohio State's lead to 13-6 with 6:08 left. Rich Spangler kicked the conversion.

OSU's defense then gave the offense a big assist. Zurbrugg threw a 18-yard bullet to tight end Sim Nelson. A Buckeye defender jarred the ball loose and defensive back William White recovered Nelson's fumble at the Michigan 37.

Byars rambled for 20 yards on the first play following White's recovery. He hit outside left guard for 3 more yards.

A delay of game penalty moved the ball back from the Wolverines' 14 to the 19. John Wooldridge, who is Byars' understudy, bolted over right tackle for 17 yards. Wooldridge bruised his back on the play and had to be taken from the field on a cart.

Byars replaced him and scored on the next play when he hammered over from the 2 to give his team a 15-point lead with 4:43 remaining.

Michigan had the ball twice more, but the OSU defense easily contained the Wolverines.

The Sound and the Fury of Bo

Bo Schembechler knew it would happen. He didn't know when, or under what condition. But the Michigan coach knew that at some point the noise generated by the largest crowd in Ohio Stadium history would become a factor in the contest.

Schembechler was positive. Hey, 90,000 or so Ohioans can raise quite a racket if it's going to help their beloved Buckeyes' chances of getting to the Rose Bowl.

So, before the start of the game Ohio State eventually won, 21-6, Schembechler told referee Otho Kortz what to expect and urged he be prepared to act accordingly.

Surely that is why Schembechler was so outraged when it finally occurred, and Kortz and his officiating crew ignored Michigan quarterback Chris Zurbrugg's plea for assistance.

It was about six minutes into the third quarter. The Wolverines were set to run the 14th play in a drive that had the faithful at Ohio Stadium gnawing their fingernails.

So when Zurbrugg brought his team to the line of scrimmage, facing a second-and-4, Buckeyes' fans set off a rumbling roar to inspire their defense.

"The crowd was really loud," Zurbrugg said. "My linemen couldn't hear. So I raised up and asked the referee for a timeout. He didn't give it to me. He just pointed at me to continue the play. The clock was running down, so I did."

But when Zurbrugg uttered the first sound of his signals, a Michigan lineman jumped and was called for illegal procedure.

Goodbye, Michigan first down. Hello, wrath of Bo.

The man performed. He was 15 yards on the field screaming at the referee. He ranted and raved on the sidelines at any official in hollering distance.

"We squandered a couple of opportunities (to win the game)," Schembechler said afterward. "But the officials sure as hell didn't help us."

"The officials on the road have to protect the quarterback. They (Ohio Stadium) flash it on the board for everyone to yell, and my quarterback kept trying to tell the official that they could not hear the signals."

Bo said he gave up on officiating in the Big Ten long ago. "They're bad officials," he said.

"All the good ones went to the NFL," he said, "and they have no good young ones coming up. Who the hell wants to be an official? Would you want to stand out there and officiate games? Hell no!"

BUCKEYES SOAK NO. 1 HAWKEYES

Columbus, Nov. 2, 1985					
Iowa	0	7	0	6 –	13
Ohio State	5	10	0	7 –	22

Buckeye leaves will be in short supply following Ohio State's dramatic 22-13 upset over No. 1 Iowa before a rain-soaked Ohio Stadium-record crowd of 90,467.

The leaves are awarded to players who make outstanding plays. There were enough of them to clean out the warehouse, despite the absence of tailback Keith Byars, who missed his sixth game of the season.

John Bozick, the Buckeyes' equipment manager who orders the leaves, will need a shopping cart to bring them back. Linebacker Chris Spielman earned the most leaves with his fine effort.

In extending its home winning streak to 20 games, Ohio State pulled itself into a first-place tie with the Hawkeyes in the Big Ten race at 4-1 with three games remaining.

OSU still must play Northwestern, Wisconsin and Michigan.

"Everyone told us that Iowa was going to pass for 1,000 yards," said Earle Bruce, OSU's jubilant coach. "But they didn't.

"That was as hard as we've played in a long, long time. It's one of the finest victories I've been associated with.

"I've never beaten a team that was No. 1 before. I think we disguised our coverages really well."

The crowd's noise and the Buckeyes' tight pass coverage bothered Iowa quarterback Chuck Long throughout the game. Long, who is the nation's leader in passing efficiency, was embarrassed by OSU's defensive backs, who call themselves the "Men of Brutality."

Long spent one of the most frustrating afternoons of his career trying to figure out what coverage they were in. He threw four interceptions and completed 17 of 34 passes for 169 yards.

Spielman intercepted two of his passes and would have had a third if he hadn't dropped Long's first attempt. He also had 19 tackles to tie Pepper Johnson for the team lead.

William White and Greg Rogan made Ohio State's two other interceptions.

Sonny Gordon also had a big play for the Buckeyes when he raced in to block Gary Kostrubala's punt in the second quarter for a safety.

Quarterback Jim Karsatos found Mike Lanese with throws of 19 and 21 yards during OSU's first

No. 1-ranked Iowa didn't care for the Columbus weather nor the treatment they received from the Buckeyes.

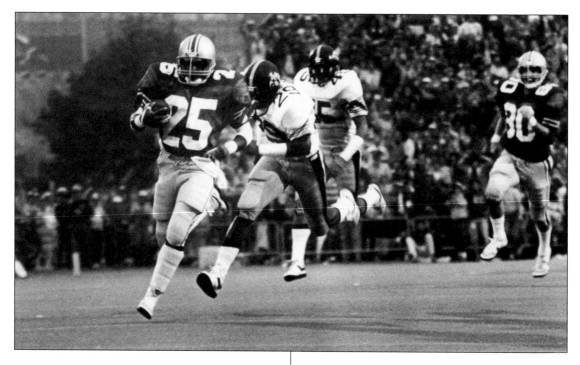

John Wooldridge (25) ran 57 yards down the middle of the field to give OSU a 12-0 lead.

scoring drive that produced Rich Spangler's 28-yard field goal.

Gordon's safety made it 5-0 Ohio State with two seconds left in the first quarter.

John Wooldridge ran 57 yards through the center of the Hawkeyes' line on a draw play to push OSU's lead to 12-0.

Nate Creer tried to stop Wooldridge with a shoestring tackle at the Iowa 10, but Wooldridge eluded his grasp.

Wooldridge and fullback George Cooper made sure the Buckeyes' running game was productive. Cooper rushed for a career-high 104 yards in 17 attempts and Wooldridge ran for 89 in nine carries.

Spangler completed the Buckeyes' first-half scoring with a 16-yard field goal that capped a

38-yard, eight play drive.

Long recovered from his erratic passing long enough to move Iowa 88 yards in 14 plays to trim OSU's lead to 15-7. Ronnie Harmon, who rushed for 127 yards in 26 carries before being hurt, played a prominent role in the drive.

Harmon opened it with a 7-yard burst over left tackle. Four plays later, Long flipped a screen pass to fullback Dave Hudson.

A gang of Buckeye defenders converged on Hudson, but he broke their tackles and ran 21 yards to the Iowa 46.

A 16-yard pass from Long to Bill Happel put the ball on the OSU 11. Hudson got 5 yards on first down. Long's pass intended for Scott Helverson was incomplete.

Harmon got 4 yards on third down. Iowa called a timeout. Fry elected to go for the touchdown. Harmon carried around left end for the score from the 3.

Long Wonders What Truck Hit Him

Iowa coach Hayden Fry and quarterback Chuck Long couldn't figure out how to beat the Buckeyes.

Chuck Long, the blond glamour boy of Iowa and the Big Ten, could not understand it.

It all happened so fast. Four hours earlier his team was unbeaten, ranked No. 1 in the nation.

He was the leading passer in the country, a strong contender for the Heisman Trophy. Last week he had thrown for six touchdowns and 399 yards.

Now it was all different. It is quite possible that Long threw away his chance at the Heisman in the rain, gloom and slippery artificial turf of Ohio Stadium.

Long was ineffective. He was intercepted four times.

"I'll probably be sick tomorrow," said the 6-4 Long. He was wearing a yellow sweater and blue sportcoat. His curly hair was uncombed. He held an orange that he didn't eat, as though trying to figure out where he was.

"I don't know what happened," Long went on. "I felt good, but it all went by so quick. It was one of my worst games."

It wasn't because Long was rushed off his feet either. The golden boy had plenty of time all day, sometimes as much as six or seven seconds. He just failed.

"I was throwing too soft at times," said Long. "I think I underestimated their defensive backs. I wasn't nervous. I was making all the reads. Maybe I was too relaxed. I have no excuses."

Long, who has been labeled a franchise passer by some pro scouts, said the Heisman Trophy, given to the season's top college player, was not in his mind. "I'm just honored to be in the running," he said. "I had the best season of my life going. But it's a far shot."

It was not the possible loss of an individual honor that bothered Long. The defeat might have cost Iowa the Big Ten championship.

"I thought we were an 11-0 team this year," Long said. "Ohio State is the front-runner now. All they have to do is win the rest of their games. But I'm still young. You learn from your mistakes. We gave the game away. I am really frustrated."

149

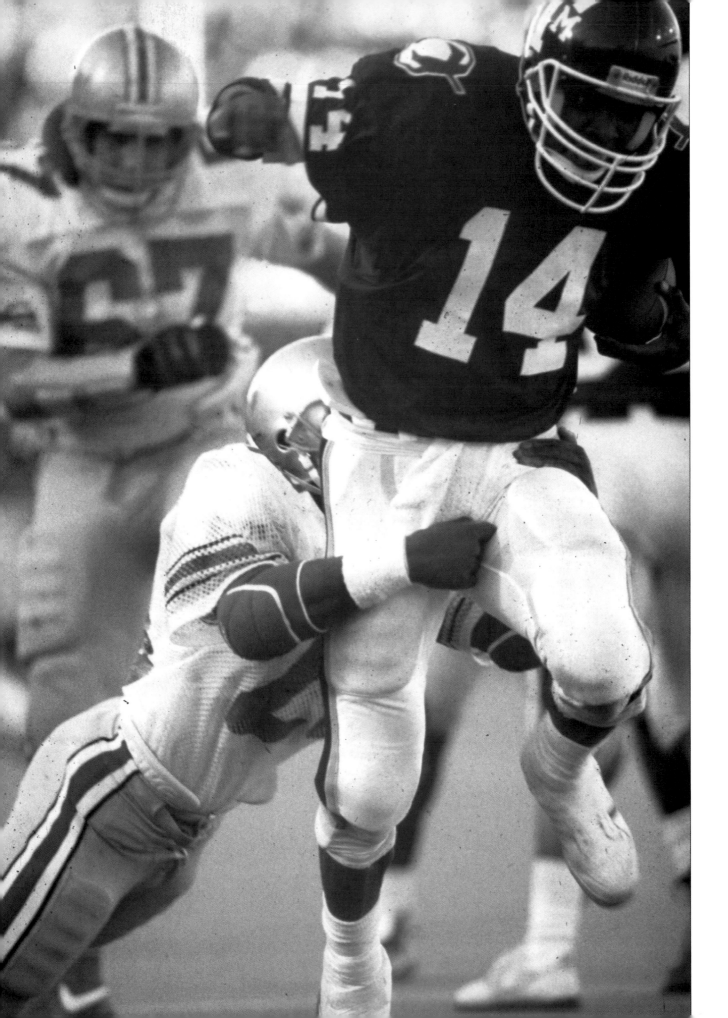

OHIO STATE SURPRISES TEXAS A&M, 28-12

Dallas, Jan. 1, 1987						
Ohio State	0	7	14	7	–	28
Texas A&M	3	3	0	6	–	12

Ohio State surprised everyone in the Cotton Bowl.

Earle Bruce, OSU coach, came out wearing a charcoal-colored suit, complete with fedora and scarlet feather. He bore a striking resemblance to the legendary mobster, Bugsy Moran.

"I thought it was about time for change in image," said Bruce, whose image in the past has been likened to oatmeal.

The team came out wearing blazing red shoes. "We wanted to do something to make the players look flashy," said Bruce.

The new-look coach, along with the new-look players, saved the biggest surprise for the 74,188 fans.

They went out and hung a 28-12 defeat on the Southwest Conference champions, Texas A&M.

"Our defense," said OSU's All-America linebacker Chris Spielman, named the game's most valuable defensive player, "felt it lost the Michigan game.

"We didn't feel good about it and we wanted to

Texas A&M QB Kevin Murray was intercepted a Cotton Bowl-record five times by the aggressive Ohio State defense.

do something about it."

They did.

OSU's defenders scored two of the team's touchdowns. They intercepted A&M's cocky quarterback, Kevin Murray, a Cotton Bowl-record five times. Spielman had two, Michael Kee, Eric Kumerow and Sonny Gordon one each.

Spielman and Kee had returns for touchdowns. Kee's TD, a 49-yarder, bettered the Cotton Bowl record held by Colorado's Byron (Whizzer) White, who had a 42-yarder in 1938.

OSU defenders limited A&M's vaunted offense to 296 total yards. The Aggies had been averaging 440 yards a game, third best in the nation.

"The difference in this game," said Bruce, "was that our defense put points on the board.

"I know there were a lot of people who said we wouldn't come back after the Michigan loss. I never believed that. I am very proud of this team."

OSU was clinging to a 7-6 halftime lead when the defense took things into its own hands.

All five interceptions were made in the second half.

The first occurred early in the third quarter. Spielman, dropping back from his linebacker spot,

Buckeye tailback Vince Workman celebrates after crossing the goal line in the third quarter.

picked off a pass intended for tight end Rod Bernstein.

Spielman, looking like a fullback, rumbled 24 yards for the first TD in his three-year career at OSU.

"Maybe it was the red shoes," he said. "I might wear them from now on."

Matt Frantz's extra point made the score 14-6.

Minutes later, rover-back Gordon got into the act, intercepting another Murray pass intended for Bernstein.

A subsequent eight-play, 59-yard drive was capped when tailback Vince Workman scored from the 8. The extra point upped the margin to 21-6.

Murray and OSU quarterback Jim Karsatos traded interceptions early in the fourth quarter. A&M rode Karsatos' interception to its only TD, with fullback Roger Vick scoring from 2 yards.

Aggies coach Jackie Sherrill decided to go for a two-point conversion, but Murray's pass into the end zone failed. OSU led, 21-12.

Kee blew the game open with 2:48 to go with his interception and touchdown run. Frantz's extra point put the Buckeyes ahead, 28-12.

The Buckeyes, who completed their 97th football season with a 10-3 record, fell behind, 3-0, when Scott Slater kicked a field goal from the 30-

yard line to conclude the Aggies' 64-yard, 10-play opening drive.

Karsatos, who completed 10 of 21 passes for 195 yards, scored OSU's first TD when he faked to tailback Jim Bryant and went over from the 3. Frantz's kick made the score 7-3.

Slater kicked at 44-yard field goal midway through the second quarter to pull the Aggies within one point.

"Ohio State is a team of big plays and they made them today," said Sherrill. "(Cris) Carter made a couple of catches that I thought might be interceptions by us.

"Instead, he caught them. It might have been a different game had we made those interceptions."

Murray, who completed 12 of 31 passes for 143 yards, didn't give OSU's defense much credit.

"It wasn't so much what Ohio State was doing," said Murray. "It was what we weren't doing.

"They didn't whip us. We were able to move the ball, but just killed ourselves."

Murray said OSU's use of Spielman was somewhat different than in the past games this season.

"They used him (Spielman) like a spy," continued Murray. "They dropped him off the line a lot more than I ever saw on their films."

Ohio State players gave Coach Earl Bruce a Texas-style ride after the Buckeyes knocked off Texas A&M.

Vick, who rushed for 113 yards on 24 carries and was named the offensive player of the game, claimed the outcome did not say anything about football in the Big Ten versus football in the SWC.

"We could come back tomorrow and beat them worse than they beat us today," he said. "Ohio State has a good team. They are big and they are quick. This game doesn't mean their conference is better than ours, though."

For one day it does, however.

OSU ERASES 31-0 DEFICIT, RALLIES TO 41-37 WIN

Minneapolis, Oct. 28, 1989						
Ohio State	0	8	10	23	–	41
Minnesota	17	14	0	6	–	37

Ohio State spent half its time digging a well of destruction and the other half furiously bailing water to remain afloat in the Big Ten title race. The Buckeyes' comeback equaled the best in college football history yesterday at the Hubert H. Humphrey Metrodome.

The Buckeyes, down 31-0 to Minnesota with five minutes left in the first half, rallied behind quarterback Greg Frey's 327 second-half passing yards to pull out a 41-37 victory.

"I've never been more proud of a football team," OSU coach John Cooper said. "We never gave up. We fought back. We kept coming back in the second half. Unfortunately, we shouldn't have put ourselves in that position."

Four first-half turnovers gave Minnesota 24 points, but its lead evaporated amid a charge that bettered OSU's previous best comeback from 24 points down against Illinois in 1984.

The Buckeyes, 3-1 in the Big Ten and 5-2 overall heading into Saturday's game at Northwestern, tied the previous best college rally of 31 points by Maryland against Miami of Florida in 1984. The Terrapins trailed by that margin with 12:35 left in the third quarter.

The Buckeyes' situation was somewhat brighter because Frey led them on an 80-yard touchdown drive to end the first half. Even so, OSU was thinking more about salvaging respectability than victory during the break.

"I told them to get out there and fight for their lives," Cooper said. "That was probably the worst half I've ever been associated with. The second half, because of the result, was probably the best."

Frey made it so, shaking off a first half in which he twice fumbled under the pressure of a Minnesota pass rush that vanished down the stretch.

"I didn't think there was any way possible they could come back," Gophers defensive end Eddie Miles said. "A game like this really hurts a team. When you're up, 31-0, it really hurts."

The ending further intensified Minnesota's pain because the Gophers nearly spoiled OSU's effort with a drive in the final 48 seconds.

"I still can't believe it," Frey said. "We've got a lot of guys who don't want to quit. We proved that today."

OSU quarterback Greg Frey gets the call he was looking for. Frey passed for 327 yards in the second half.

FOR OSU, EIGHT IS NOT ENOUGH

I t was the most miserable day in Ohio Stadium in recent memory, and for all but a handful of the 95,060 in attendance, also the most enjoyable.

Intermittent snow and rain, mixed with 34-degree temperatures, proved only minor annoyances to a crowd that snuggled up to third-ranked Ohio State's 24-6 victory over 12th-ranked Penn State and the visions it inspired at the Horseshoe.

Outslugging the Nittany Lions on a field turned treacherous by the elements, OSU slammed to a

Columbus, Oct. 30, 1993						
Penn State	6	0	0	0	–	6
Ohio State	7	10	7	0	–	24

Despite the snow and the Penn State defense, Raymont Harris rushed for a career-high 151 yards.

157

17-6 halftime lead and never wavered in drawing closer to its first Rose Bowl in nine seasons.

Now 8-0 overall and 5-0 in the Big Ten, the Buckeyes take a one-game lead into the game at Wisconsin, which shares second place with Indiana and Illinois at 4-1.

Because of its victory at Illinois, Ohio State can clinch a Rose Bowl berth with victories over Wisconsin and Indiana the next two weeks, regardless of the result of the regular-season finale at Michigan on Nov. 20.

"I can smell a faint smell of roses," said OSU tailback Raymont Harris, whose career-high 32 carries yielded a career-high 151 yards rushing and one touchdown. "But right now, I smell Badgers, and the roses smell a lot better."

Jason Simmons drags down Penn State quarterback Kerry Collins, who struggled all afternoon.

That's because the fragrance of New Year's Day in Pasadena is considerably more appealing to the Buckeyes than a return trip to Camp Randall Stadium, where Wisconsin inflicted a 20-16 loss on unbeaten OSU the fourth week of last season.

"I'm tremendously pleased with this victory," OSU coach John Cooper said. "But I know Wisconsin beat Michigan, so it's going to be showdown time in Madison."

"They are just too tough," said Penn State coach Joe Paterno, whose hopes for a Rose Bowl appearance in his team's first year in the Big Ten are a long shot at 2-2 in the conference and 5-2 overall. "Their offensive line was something we just could not belly up to."

For Cooper, Gee, Perfection Sweet

The Penn State Nittany Lions went home from their first Big Ten visit to Ohio Stadium looking as if they'd been dragged behind a horse from the state line.

John Cooper's best day of coaching outside of Arizona produced a 24-6 triumph and a fourth-quarter press box tour by Ohio State president E. Gordon Gee that was the equivalent of a home run trot, though far slower.

With eight wins behind him, three against ranked teams, Cooper has reason to feel just as satisfied as his boss.

When asked if such a public drubbing of Joe Paterno and his Nittany Lions compared to anything in his coaching portfolio, Cooper needed all of a millisecond to answer.

"Here?" he said. "Probably not. Not at this stage of the season with everything on the line against a good football team. No, probably not."

Probably not. Fact is, there isn't much in the past to compare favorably with Ohio State's fifth consecutive conference victory. And now we interrupt this dream season for an even dreamier thought, the battle cry sounded by Cooper that next week is the "showdown time up in Madison."

Falling snow was the first hint that the Buckeyes aren't in Pasadena yet. But the possibility is no longer accompanied by a laugh track.

"Every team we play is in our way to get to the Rose Bowl," said Ohio State guard Jason Winrow. "We're not going to let anybody stand in our way."

The local police force defended the goal posts better than Penn State managed at various times yesterday. And offensively, the goal posts stood as the only avenue of scoring for Penn State, which managed one field goal on which kicker Craig Fayak forgot to call "bank" and a 49-yarder that would've been good from at least 49 yards and a half-inch.

"At halftime, I thought we could get back into the game," Penn State coach Joe Paterno said. "But they are just too tough. I repeat, Ohio State is a very good football team."

After five years in which thoughts of the Rose Bowl faded by the first snowfall, neither snow nor rain nor Penn State could keep Ohio State from making another one of its rounds in this dominant Big Ten season.

Last year's tie against Michigan might've been the greatest lifeline ever tossed a coach.

Cooper's Buckeyes are 8-0 for the first time in 14 seasons.

This year, a win over Michigan is expected. And the only tie that's acceptable is Gordon Gee's neckwear of choice.

OHIO STATE ROCKS MICHIGAN

A s they waded through the celebrants littering the playing surface and attacking the Ohio Stadium goal posts, the unfamiliar sweetness of a victory over Michigan began to settle upon the Ohio State Buckeyes.

It had pride pumping in their chests and pleasure in full flower on their faces.

It also had pain throbbing in the right hand of OSU coach John Cooper.

Years from now, when time has fermented the Buckeyes' 22-6 victory and distilled it into a single memory, Coopers' halftime haymaker at his locker room blackboard might outlive anything that transpired yesterday in the old Horseshoe.

Columbus, Nov. 19, 1994						
Michigan	0	3	3	0	–	6
Ohio State	2	10	0	10	–	22

Ohio State Coach John Cooper didn't hide his emotions after his Buckeyes ripped Michigan.

OSU quarterback Bob Hoying sticks the ball in the end zone against the visiting Wolverines.

"That got a real spark under us," offensive tackle Korey Stringer said. "Coach Cooper came in, and he was as excited as I've ever seen him. He was so fired up, the next thing you know, he hauled off and knocked the blackboard out. He put a good dent in it, too."

That move, as out of character for the mild-mannered Cooper as the victory was to his previous 0- 5-1 record as OSU coach against the Wolverines, lent further urgency to Ohio State's first victory in the series since 1987.

"That really showed us how much he wanted to pull out the victory," OSU tailback Eddie George said. "He's usually laid back and calm. He's not usually into emotional speeches, but that definitely pumped us up."

"I don't look at it like I beat Michigan," Cooper said. "Just like in past years, I didn't really feel like I had lost to Michigan. Our football team beat

Michigan today. This football program beat Michigan, and it was an outstanding Michigan team."

"This was a defensive struggle," OSU quarterback Bob Hoying said. "Our defense did a good job getting us the ball in good field position, and a couple of times we were able to take advantage of it."

Scott Terna's first-quarter punt pushed the Wolverines to their 1-yard line, where quarterback Todd Collins stumbled retreating from center for a safety and a 2-0 OSU lead.

A 40-yard drive for a touchdown off the subse-

quent free kick provided a 9-0 lead, but that would not have happened without George's 6-yard run on fourth-and-1 from the Michigan 31.

Another fourth-down conversion, this time a Hoying pass to Joey Galloway at the Wolverines' 29, fed a 64-yard drive to Josh Jackson's 26-yard field goal and a 12-0 margin six minutes before the half.

Michigan reduced the deficit to 12-6 on two 22-yard Remy Hamilton field goals, and was threatening a further advance on the lead when OSU's special teams arose again.

"We needed somebody to make plays," Cooper said. "When Marlon (Kerner) came off the corner and blocked the field goal, it was a big, big momentum play for us."

Only two snaps earlier, Michigan wide receiver Amani Toomer had beaten Kerner badly to break free in the end zone, but Collins' pass led Toomer out of bounds.

"I dodged a bullet there," Kerner said, "so I knew I had to do something to make it up."

He did so by sweeping in to smother Hamilton's kick, delayed by a high snap, and send the ball bouncing toward midfield.

Jackson's subsequent 36-yard field goal boosted OSU's edge to 15-6 with 11:22 remaining, enticing the Wolverines to turn to Collins' passing skills.

His next pass glanced off nose guard Luke Fickell's extended arm and hung lazily for him to intercept at the Michigan 16.

"It's something you dream about every day," Fickell said. "You visualize yourself making a play like that."

George took five carries to convert the turnover into a touchdown and give the 93,869 in attendance an eight-minute head start on their post-game revelry.

GEORGE RUNS WILD AS BUCKEYES DEFEAT IRISH

So, it turns out, lightning can strike twice in the same place.

OK, same place, different sideline.

The identical momentum swing that fixed Ohio State and Notre Dame's first meeting 60 years ago returned to Ohio Stadium yesterday, only this time with wildly different allegiances.

What made winners of the Fighting Irish in 1935 swung the Buckeyes into action midway through the third quarter and triggered their getaway to a 45-26 victory in front of a record crowd of 95,537.

"I don't know how much anybody paid for tickets," OSU coach John Cooper said, "But I guarantee you they got their money's worth."

Irish fans probably crowed the same lyrics 60 years ago, when their team erased a 13-0 fourth-quarter deficit in an 18-13 comeback win touted by some as the game of the century.

Coach Lou Holtz's surprise return to the Irish sideline raised the specter of just that type of Irish magic.

This time, holding a 20-14 third-quarter lead

Notre Dame had trouble bringing down Eddie George, who rushed for 207 yards on 35 carries.

and about to gain possession of an OSU punt, the Irish went fumble, interception, fumble in a three-turnover parlay that proved decisive.

"We shouldn't have lost the way we did," Irish quarterback Ron Powlus said. "If we lost, it should have been on a field goal late. We weren't beaten badly. We just beat ourselves."

Back to receive a punt near his own 20 with 6:33 left in the third quarter, Notre Dame's Emmett Mosely signaled for a fair catch, ran forward to let the football sail beyond him, then circled backward and stuck out his arm.

OSU's Dean Kruezer tracked the fumble at the Irish 19 and quarterback Bob Hoying snapped a 15-yard touchdown to Rickey Dudley three plays later for the go-ahead score, 21-20.

"The momentum shifted 1,000 degrees to them," Mosely said. "Ohio State is a great football team. You can't afford to make those kinds of mistakes. That turnover started things downhill."

Powlus momentarily rallied the Irish with a 56-yard completion to Derrick Mayes. The gain took them to the OSU 32, within range of a go-ahead field goal, before another mistake intruded.

Going for Mayes on third-and-10 at the OSU

32, Powlus' receiver ran inside on a pattern designed for the sideline and Shawn intercepted for the Buckeyes at their 11.

Three plays later, OSU was in the end zone again, with Hoying's 12-yard pass to Terry Glenn going for an 82-yard touchdown thanks to Glenn's turbo boost.

"When I caught the ball, I was thinking about getting the first down," Glenn said. "But as I started running, I looked out of the corner of my eye and I saw No. 15 (Allen Rossum) chasing me.

"This guy was supposed to be some kind of track all-American in high school, so I thought, 'Let's see how fast he is.' I just turned on the jets and got the touchdown."

The resultant 28-20 OSU lead instilled enough panic in Powlus that he rushed from under center on Notre Dame's next snap and lost the football.

OSU's Matt Bonhaus dove on the fumble at the Irish 14 and Eddie George hammered in from there, again in three plays, for a 35-20 lead five seconds into the fourth quarter.

"They made the mistakes and we capitalized," George said. "That was the difference."

If the turnovers weren't, George's 61-yard run after Notre Dame pulled within 35-26 certainly was.

Randy Kinder brought the Irish that close with a 13-yard run with 12:55 remaining.

But George, on the Buckeyes' next snap, broke free on a sweep left and ran to the Notre Dame 19.

His second touchdown shortly thereafter com-

Mike Vrabel takes a break during the Buckeyes' 45-26 victory over visiting Notre Dame.

pleted a 35-carry, 207-yard day, the fourth 200-yard game of his career and the second this season.

"Ohio State's big plays were disastrous for us," Holtz said. "Give Ohio State all the credit in the world. We knew we had to play error-free football and we couldn't do it."

The Irish were flawless for a time, using the very ball-control game plan OSU expected to battle.

"He's a master," Cooper said of Holtz. "He did

Wide receiver Terry Glenn races to the goal line on an 82-yard TD run.

a good job keeping us off balance. He had us sort of second-guessing ourselves defensively."

Notre Dame drove 95 yards on its second possession in a 16-play drive that consumed 7:21 of the first quarter and foreshadowed the remainder of the first half.

BUCKEYES OUTDUEL PENN STATE, 28-25

State College, Pa., Oct. 7, 1995						
Ohio State	0	14	7	7	–	28
Penn State	10	0	8	7	–	25

The circumstances of Ohio State's 28-25 victory suggest there might be a force at work for the fifth-ranked Buckeyes.

A G-force.

Unleashing flanker Terry Glenn and tailback Eddie George at alternate moments of despair, OSU overcame trouble both early and late in a win that could prove the defining moment of its season.

Glenn's two touchdown receptions and 175 receiving yards fed a comeback from a 10-0 first-quarter deficit to a 21-10 lead.

But it wasn't until George's 6-yard touchdown run with 1:42 remaining erased a 25-21 deficit that Coach John Cooper could breathe comfortably.

"What a great victory," said Cooper, whose Buckeyes rose to 5-0 overall, 1-0 in the Big Ten. "I don't believe I've ever coached a football team that fought off as much adversity and deserved to win."

The 12th-ranked Nittany Lions appeared poised for the upset when Bob Hoying's fourth-down pass to Glenn flew incomplete at the Penn State 15 with 5:05 left.

"We just knew we had to get the ball back," OSU nose guard Luke Fickell said. "Our offense has been great all year. We knew if we got it back, they would score."

So, despite having yielded touchdown drives of 84 and 86 yards in the second half, OSU's defense arose to force its second straight three-and-out series and set the offense up at its 42 with 3:10 remaining.

"We knew it was our one chance and that we had to make the most of it," George said.

"We'd been moving the ball all day. Now we really had to make some plays."

No one made more plays than Glenn, who had nine receptions on an array of leaping, diving catches that belied a pregame aggravation of a lingering shoulder injury.

Much of Glenn's freedom came courtesy of George, whose rushing success this season caused Penn State to commit heavily to crowding the line of scrimmage.

"It was obvious they came in with the idea of stopping the run," Hoying said. "To do that, they had to give up the pass, so that's what we took."

Penn State's preoccupation with the run allowed Hoying to complete 22 of his first 33 passes for 309 yards, but the two biggest completions in his career-best performance were yet to come.

On third-and-10 from the OSU 42, Hoying found Buster Tillman alone along the left sideline for a 13-yard gain and fresh momentum.

That took the Buckeyes to the Penn State 45, where Hoying again went downfield, this time to tight end Ricky Dudley for 32 yards to the Lions' 13.

"They had a linebackers covering me and I had the advantage," said Dudley, who ran the same route for a 25-yard touchdown in the first half. "He took the wrong angle to cover me and when Bob saw that, he got me the ball."

Hoying put the throw over the shoulder of linebacker Gerald Filardi, whose coverage on Dudley suffered only from his failure to turn and observe the football as it passed beside him.

"After that, there was no doubt we were going to score," Dudley said.

Not with 2:40 left and George in the backfield aching for atonement.

His first-quarter fumble led to a Penn State field goal that put the Buckeyes in a 10-0 hole.

And only an incorrect call that George was down on a third-quarter carry spared George another fumble.

"There's nothing I can do about it," Penn State coach Joe Paterno said. "I'm sure (the official) wanted to call it the right way. If he blew it, he blew it."

Hoying seized upon the break by hitting Glenn

on the next play for a 37-yard touchdown and a 21-10 lead.

But with the Buckeyes trailing, 25-21, George wasn't about to tempt another turnover.

With both hands on the football, he drove through the middle for 7 yards to the Penn State 6.

Then, following blocks from Dudley and Nicky Sualua around left end, George had no fear of fumbling as he scored the game-winner untouched.

"They were looking for me all day," said George, who finished with 105 yards on 24 carries. "They were stunting and twisting and it made the yards really tough. I'm just glad I was able to get one in at the end and we were able to come out with the victory."

Wally Richardson's 18-yard pass to Freddie Scott and a 12-yard completion to John Whitman took Penn State to midfield with 1:30 left.

The Lions ran low on precision there, falling into a fourth-and-19 predicament when OSU's Luke Fickell broke through and forced a Richardson fumble in the backfield.

"I'm obviously proud of our offense, but the credit for this one goes to the defense," Cooper said. "When we had to have the ball back late in the game, the pass rush was there and the defense came through when we needed it."

"What a great victory. I don't believe I've ever coached a football team that fought off as much adversity and deserved to win."

— OHIO STATE COACH
JOHN COOPER

GREATEST MOMENTS IN OHIO STATE FOOTBALL HISTORY

GEORGE CARRIES THE LOAD IN BLOWOUT

Columbus, Nov. 11, 1995

Illinois	0	0	3	0	–	3
Ohio State	14	3	21	3	–	41

The expanse of material between the 2 and the 7 on Eddie George's Ohio State football jersey appears too narrow to accommodate any additional cargo.

But his entire team fit between those digits yesterday in Ohio Stadium, climbing aboard George's record-setting and perhaps Heisman Trophy-clinching performance in a piggyback thrill ride to a 41-3 victory over Illinois.

"I've never seen a better individual effort than Eddie put on out there," OSU coach John Cooper said.

Neither has anyone with scarlet-and-gray loyalties, for George's 313 rushing yards pushed Keith Byars' single-game record of 274 yards off the page and left his own mark in Ohio State history.

Byars' signature performance against the Illini 11 years ago featured a 67-yard touchdown run without a shoe.

George gave the 92,639 in attendance a 64-yard scoring sprint on OSU's first play of the second half to remember him by.

"I just wanted to close the door immediately," George said.

Coming on the heels of an Illinois field goal to open the third quarter, the first of George's three touchdowns ended all worries that OSU would struggle without flanker Terry Glenn.

He sat out because of a slight shoulder separa-

Eddie George ran for 313 yards against the Illini and locked up the 1995 Heisman Trophy with this outstanding performance.

tion suffered last week at Minnesota, but the Buckeyes never missed Glenn's game-breaking talents.

They just looked elsewhere for the same

OSU quarterback Bob Hoying got plenty of time to pass thanks to a great effort by the Buckeye front line.

ammunition and easily improved to 10-0 overall and 9-0 in the Big Ten, one-half game behind Northwestern entering a Saturday home game with Indiana.

"Without Terry, Eddie really stepped up his game," quarterback Bob Hoying said. "I didn't know if we would have too many big plays without Terry,

but we just got them on the ground instead."

None were bigger than George's quick strike to start OSU's second half.

Though nose tackle Paul Marshall had him 5 yards deep in the backfield, George stepped out of that tackle and sped through a seam that led him down the left sideline and into the end zone for a 24-3 advantage.

"I came through plugging the gap and had him clear in my sights," Marshall said. "I just missed him. I feel bad about the play. We had some momentum going. I blame myself. I should have made it. It was typical of the day."

Also typical of the frustrations of Marshall's more-heralded defensive teammates.

Butkus Award finalists Simeon Rice and Kevin Hardy caused relatively little havoc at linebacker, combining for seven tackles and one sack.

"Looking at the film, I wondered how we were going to get 20 yards," George said of the total Iowa managed on the ground against Illinois last week. "We just wanted to go out and establish some kind of running game.

"I figured it was going to be close all day, but we came out with the attitude of getting the job done."

Notice of that came early, after Illinois pinned OSU at its 1 on a punt five minutes after kickoff.

Having suffered a Hoying interception already, the Buckeyes went to George to escape their own end and reaped 24- and 39-yard runs that fed a six-play scoring drive — all of it on the ground.

Dimitrious Stanley's 14-yard touchdown catch and a John Jackson field goal of 20 yards also traced to George's 180 first-half rushing yards before he began assaulting the end zone himself.

"Eddie George was just spectacular," Illini coach Lou Tepper said. "Eddie George was just a nightmare."

Tepper's nightmare worsened in the third quarter, starting with George's 64-yard scoring sprint.

That gave OSU a 24-3 lead and put him in range of Byars' record, which fell on a 13-yard touchdown run with 3:07 left in the quarter.

Damon Moore's interception and subsequent return gave George time for another TD before the quarter ended, this one coming on a 13-yard pass from Hoying.

That gave George three third-quarter scores to

Ohio State wide receiver Rickey Dudley (80) outruns an Illinois defender.

go with his 105 rushing yards in the quarter — more of both totals than Illinois' defense had allowed per game in achieving its second-place ranking in the Big Ten.

"Big No. 27, wow, he came to play today and did a great job with every opportunity he had," Cooper said of George. "If Eddie George isn't the finest football player in the nation and deserving of the Heisman Trophy, I don't know who is."

Heisman Can Call Columbus Its Hometown

I t happened in Hollywood, where thousands of theatrical tales have hatched.

No meringue sweetens this one, though.

Its panache lies in its purity.

For while it is, most assuredly, a charming story, it is also a true story.

Seems the bride of Les Horvath one day asked him to please remove, from the living room of their Los Angeles home, the lone trophy he desired to display from his collegiate athletic career.

The bronze statue of a football player posed in a stiff-arm stance just didn't mesh with Mrs. Horvath's tastes, but her husband protested on the grounds that this was a special award few possessed.

Satisfied with that explanation, she relented until visits to their friends, Mr. and Mrs. Thomas Harmon and Mr. and Mrs. Felix "Doc" Blanchard, turned up

Archie Griffin is the only player in college football history to win the Heisman Trophy twice.

*Versatile Vic Janowicz won the Heisman Trophy,
as a junior, in 1950.*

the exact same trophy with the exact same "Down-town Athletic Club of New York City" engraving.

"Les," she said on the drive home from the Blan-chards, "you told me that football trophy of yours was really something special, but it turns out that everyone we know has one."

What Horvath did for the Buckeyes, winning the Heisman Trophy in 1944, Vic Janowicz would also accomplish in 1950, as would Howard (Hopalong) Cassady in 1955, Archie Griffin in 1974 and 1975 and Eddie George in 1995.

That six-pack of Heisman hardware gives OSU more such honorees than any school except Notre

Dame, creating a brotherhood within a brotherhood that will forever bind Horvath, Janowicz, Cassady, Griffin and George.

"The thing that's special about the Heisman is the camaraderie you enjoy with the other winners," said Cassady, who led OSU to the national cham-pionship in 1954, the year before winning the award by a 1,477-vote margin over TCU's Jim Swink.

Griffin is the only two-time Heisman winner and, therefore, is the most accomplished player in Ohio State history.

The only OSU Heisman recipient to make All-Amer-ica three times, Griffin shattered school, conference and NCAA career rushing marks in gaining 5,589 yards and taking the Buckeyes to four straight Rose Bowls.

"Being a Heisman winner means a whole heck

of a lot to me," Griffin said. "I know I wouldn't have been able to go to some of the places I've gone or speak to some of the people I've spoken to without being a Heisman Trophy winner. That award opens doors for you, but more important- ly, it identifies you with a group of people who took their talent and developed it through hard work."

No OSU Heisman

winner may have been more athletically gifted that Janowicz, and none worked harder to achieve their success than George.

"Vic had to be one of the finest athletes ever to play at Ohio State," said Walt Klevay, a teammate dur- ing Janowicz's three varsity seasons from 1949-51.

Heisman voters rewarded him for his 938 total offensive yards and 16 touchdowns — not to men- tion an against-the-elements field goal from 27 yards in the 1950 Snow Bowl against Michigan — and made Janowicz a better than two-to-one winner over Southern Methodist's Kyle Rote in the balloting.

"I can't imagine Ohio State ever having a more versatile player," said Marv Homan, who began call- ing OSU games on radio in 1949, Janowicz's sopho- more season. George's path to the Heisman was decidedly different, emerging out of oblivion.

That's pretty much the place he inhabited on the depth chart most of his freshman season and all of his sophomore year after losing two fumbles on the Illinois 1-yard line in a bitter defeat five games into his career.

"That Illinois game my freshman year was the

Howard (Hopalong) Cassady won the Heisman Trophy in 1955 and appeared on Ed Sullivan's show in New York.

fuel to my fire," George said.

Having scored only two of 12 touchdowns as a junior from more than 6 yards away, he scored eight of his 25 rushing touchdowns as a senior from 10 or more yards, including runs of 51, 64 and 87 yards.

All that contributed to his OSU single-season record of 1,927 rushing yards, with the highlight a single-game mark of 314 that settled his long-stand- ing grudge against Illinois.

"I've been in this business for 35 years, and Eddie George has the best work ethic of any player I've ever been around," OSU coach John Cooper said. "He set the standard here that all our players try to live up to. He was the heart and soul of our team that year."

Every Heisman winner is, but perhaps none more so than Horvath.

His career was supposedly over after the 1942 sea- son, but with America fully engaged in the war effort, a scarcity of players on the college level emerged.

177

That convinced the NCAA to allow freshman eligibility for the 1944 season, and also to grant an additional year of eligibility to anyone who had been ineligible as a freshman earlier in their career.

Horvath played a team-high 402 of 540 possible minutes as OSU went 9-0 and won the national civilian championship, finishing second in the polls only to No. 1 Army.

Such success wasn't forecast for a team that started three freshmen in its backfield, but the 24-year-old Horvath carried OSU's youth via his 924 rushing yards, 344 passing yards and team-high 72 points.

Cassady served immediate notice as the heir to Horvath's and Janowicz's Heisman legacy by bounding off the bench to score three touchdowns against Indiana in his 1952 debut as a 150-pound freshman.

He remained in the lineup every game thereafter and gave OSU its first outright Big Ten championship since Horvath's final year.

With Cassady at left halfback, Bobby Watkins at right halfback and Hubert Bobo at fullback, the Buckeyes had the top three rushers in the Big Ten.

Ironically, Cassady's 5.4-yards per carry average was the lowest of the group, but there was never any question who was their leader.

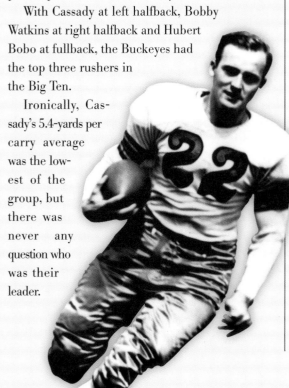

That quality shone the brightest when second-ranked Wisconsin led fourth-ranked OSU, 7-3, and was driving for another score in the fifth game of the 1954 season.

Cassady intercepted, and his 88-yard touchdown return earned Coach Woody Hayes' praise as "the most spectacular play in 20 years of football in our stadium."

The victory over Wisconsin elevated OSU to No.1 in the polls and the Buckeyes stayed there, thanks to a come-from-behind victory over Michigan.

Cassady sparked that with a 52-yard run on Ohio State's winning 99-yard touchdown drive. His 92 rushing yards in the 20-7 Rose Bowl victory over USC sealed the national championship.

A first-team All-American and a third-place finisher in the Heisman voting that year, Cassady was one of only four starters OSU returned in 1955.

Fortunately for him, one of the others was All-American lineman Jim Parker, so Cassady's rushing total increased from 701 yards as a junior to 958 as a senior.

"We couldn't go to the Rose Bowl that year because of the no-repeat rule," Cassady said. "I wanted to win the Heisman, just like I wanted to win everything I could, whether it was games, All-American honors for the second time, or whatever. It wasn't hyped then like it is now, but everybody knew it was the best award."

Cassady became its runaway recipient by closing his career at home in the season's next-to-last game with a 45-yard touchdown run on his first carry and two more scores that day.

Michigan certainly didn't have the recipe to stop him, for Cassady gained 146 yards on 28 carries the following week to give OSU another

In 1944, Les Horvath became Ohio State's first Heisman Trophy award winner. He had 1,248 yards of total offense.

Big Ten championship.

Of course, no one specialized in frustrating Michigan more than Griffin, whose talents led Ohio State to Pasadena every year of his career.

The Wolverines went 38-4-2 over that span, but were 0-3-1 against OSU.

Griffin was the primary reason, getting a 30-yard touchdown for the game-winner as a freshman, rushing for 163 yards as a sophomore, 111 yards as a junior and 46 as a senior.

That latter total stopped Griffin's still-existing NCAA record of consecutive 100-yard games at 31, but it didn't stop the Buckeyes from a still-unmatched streak of Rose Bowl appearances.

That team success and Griffin's then-NCAA

Eddie George turned on the jets his senior year, scoring eight of his 25 touchdowns from 10 yards or more.

career rushing record of 5,589 yards, nearly 1,000 more than the previous mark owned by Cornell's Ed Marinaro, made him a better-than-1,000-vote Heisman winner for the second straight season.

Griffin said, "Everywhere I went that year, people were asking me, 'Can you win it again?' Hey, I didn't know if I could or not. I knew they'd never given it to the same person twice, but I sure knew I wanted to win it. I wanted that second Heisman."

Even Mrs. Horvath would agree, they make a nice pair of bookends.

BUCKEYES OVERPOWER IRISH

Ghosts and mystique and Irish luck no doubt have their merits. It's just that speed and power and unforgiving blitzes are sometimes better.

Particularly when wrapped in a fortuitous yellow flag.

No. 4 Ohio State unleashed each of those weapons yesterday in a 29-16 throttling of fifth-ranked Notre Dame that was every bit the sequel of the 45-26 beating OSU applied last season.

Although the margin wasn't as wide this time, the thoroughness of the Buckeyes' superiority was just as evident until some fourth-quarter theatrics by the Irish.

The vaunted echoes of the Rockne, Leahy and Parseghian eras that awoke in support of so many Notre Dame comebacks of bygone season stirred only briefly yesterday, but were silenced by a hold-

South Bend, Ind., Sept 29, 1996						
Ohio State	12	10	7	0	–	29
Notre Dame	7	0	3	6	–	16

ing penalty that erased Autry Denson's 90-yard punt return for an apparent touchdown with 3:35 remaining.

With that score, the Irish would have been within a touchdown of yet another storybook finish.

Instead, OSU basked in the afterglow of a victory that will join its 1995 triumph over the Irish as regal bookends in the scarlet-and-gray archives.

"It does not get any better than this," said John Cooper, clutching the game ball from his 150th career victory, in his 100th game as Ohio State's head coach. "Not many teams come in here in this environment and beat an outstanding team like Notre Dame."

In so doing, the Buckeyes eloquently legitimized their 70-7 and 72-0 frolics over Rice and Pittsburgh and boldly declared their Rose Bowl and national championship intentions.

That dual message was delivered in a forceful duet, spoken by Ohio State's offense and its defense.

Tailback Pepe Pearson rushed for 173 yards and two touchdowns, one of which he set up with a 26-yard pass reception.

Quarterback Stanley Jackson was just as good, completing 9 of 15 passes for 154 yards and nimbly avoiding Notre Dame's pursuit throughout.

Irish quarterback Ron Powlus was not allowed to escape by an OSU defense that blitzed unrelentingly from all angles to keep Notre Dame from being sharp on offense.

"Those blitzes don't work unless you stop the run," said linebacker Greg Bellisari, whose 14 tackles led Ohio State. "We got them in second-

Ohio State's relentless blitzing defense kept Notre Dame quarterback Ron Powlus (3) running for his life.

and-long and third-and-long all day, and then we did a great job getting after them with the blitz."

Notre Dame's rushing game, which averaged 242 yards in its three previous victories, managed just 126 against the Buckeyes.

Safeties Rob Kelly and Damon Moore had a hand in that success thanks to the cumbersome coverage of cornerbacks Ty Howard and Shawn Springs, who neutralized Notre Dame's receivers with one-on-one coverage.

"We knew they were a good running team," Moore said of the Irish, "so we put Ty and Shawn on an island and just said, 'Have a nice day.' Then Rob and I just concentrated on stopping the run."

Notre Dame had no similar strategy or ability to stop OSU, which bruised to a 22-7 halftime lead thanks to a 283-93 edge in total offense.

"I thought we could do some of the same things we've done (against Rice and Pitt) against them," Jackson said. "Pepe had (173) yards, so I think that proves how good our offensive line is. I think we have the best offensive line in the country. I think we proved that."

The first sign of OSU's domination came not from the trenches, but from its special teams. Dimitrious Stanley's 85-yard return of the opening kickoff positioned the Buckeyes for a touchdown inside the first two minutes.

Ohio State Coach John Cooper said, "It doesn't get much better than this," after OSU defeated Notre Dame.

Pearson slipped a tackle in the backfield to score from the 3-yard line, and only a botched extra point allowed Notre Dame the leeway for a brief and solitary possession of the lead.

The 7-6 margin the Irish eventually enjoyed came after an Ohio State turnover at the Buckeyes' 15-yard line, which Powlus cashed with a 2-yard pass to Marc Edwards. The point-after provided a cushion that lasted two minutes and 28 seconds.

The Buckeyes faces one second down and no third downs on that 80-yard possession, chewing up yardage in chain-moving increments until Jackson flipped a 3-yard pass to Matt Calhoun for the score.

Jackson's try for the 2-point conversion run failed, but OSU soon sent its lead to 15-7 when backup quarterback Joe Germaine directed a 68-yard drive to the 7.

Josh Jackson's 24-yard field goal ended that possession, and when Notre Dame punted after three plays, the Buckeyes came back for more.

With Jackson again at the controls and 2:16 left in the half, OSU went 84 yards in six plays and scored with 1:22 to spare.

Pearson's 1-yard run ballooned the lead to 22-7, coming on the heels of his catch and cross-field run on which he avoided three tackles for a 26-yard gain.

Notre Dame tried to answer to start the second half, but settled for a field goal after moving to the 8.

Tailback Pepe Pearson ran for 173 yards and scored two touchdowns to lead Ohio State.

D.J. Jones' 14-yard touchdown catch at 1:44 of the third quarter sent OSU's lead to 29-10, making Notre Dame's mountain too high to climb, particularly without Denson's punt return.

"When that one was called back," Holtz said, "all chance of winning was over."

OHIO STATE ROLLS OVER PENN STATE

Columbus, Oct. 5, 1996

Penn State	0	0	0	7	–	7
Ohio State	10	14	7	7	–	38

The nameless jerseys and logoless helmets are so distinctively indistinctive that Penn State stands apart from all other football programs.

Without that signatureless brand yesterday in Ohio Stadium, it would have been difficult distinguishing the fourth-ranked Nittany Lions from the bottom-feeders at Rice and Pittsburgh who preceded them under the wheel of Ohio State's runaway locomotive.

The third-ranked Buckeyes turned yet another "game for the ages" into just another Saturday afternoon stroll by inflicting a 38-7 facial that reigns as Penn State's worst loss since a 44-7 hammering by Notre Dame in 1984.

That's the same Notre Dame that was supposed to engage in an epic struggle with OSU last week in South Bend before the Buckeyes laid a 29-16 thunderclap on the then-No. 5 Fighting Irish.

"You don't very often get an opportunity to play two Top-5 teams back-to-back," Ohio State coach John Cooper said. "For us to win both games as convincingly as we did is very satisfying."

OSU's domination was so thorough that it outgained the Lions, 74-32, in the first half, en route to a 24-0 lead.

The Buckeyes tacked on another touchdown and tipped their total offense advantage to 423-133 by the end of three quarters, then sent in the same substitutes who baby-sat the 70-7 and 72-0 destructions of Rice and Pittsburgh.

"We just got a good whipping every which way," Penn State coach Joe Paterno said. "They played with more poise and more confidence than we did."

The Nittany Lions' defense that had allowed only 27 points in five previous victories proved no impediment to OSU, which rode a burgeoning cast to the surprising blowout.

Tailback Pepe Pearson rushed for 141 yards and one touchdown, and quarterbacks Stanley Jackson and Joe Germaine were typically efficient, throwing two touchdown passes apiece and splitting 215 passing yards.

Their favorite target was flanker Dimitrious Stanley, who grabbed a touchdown pass from each quarterback. OSU's tag team fullbacks, Matt Keller and Matt Calhoun, also caught one scoring pass apiece.

"This team has an awful lot of weapons," Pearson said. "There isn't just one guy who can beat you. It's a lot of different guys, and you never know who it's going to be next."

Stanley's first touchdown set the tone for Penn State's frustration, tracing to a mistake in coverage on the Buckeyes' second series that allowed him to gain more elbow room than anyone in the Horseshoe.

"I don't know what they were doing." said Jack-

Tailback Pepe Pearson led an explosive OSU offense with 141 yards rushing and one touchdown.

son, who lofted the 42-yard scoring pass to complete a three-play, 69-yard drive. "I just dropped back and saw him wide open. I was just hoping I didn't overthrow it."

He didn't.

Billed as a severe test for OSU's run defense, the Lions all but abandoned the avenue by which they had averaged 231 yards per game once the Buckeyes increased their lead to 10-0 late in the first quarter.

Penn State tailback Curtis Enis carried only four more times the remainder of the half, while quarterback Wally Richardson went a woeful 3 of 11 and failed to move his team beyond midfield even once.

"I thought they were going to try to establish the run," OSU safety Rob Kelly said. "They did it a little in the first quarter, but after that, it was invisible."

So, apparently, was Keller coming out of the Buckeyes' backfield.

His 24-yard catch-and-run after a simple swing pass from Jackson provided a 17-0 Ohio State lead at 9:03 of the second quarter.

Keller went in untouched on that play to complete an 80-yard drive on which the Buckeyes converted a third-and-10, a third-and-2 and a fourth-and-2, all via passes from Jackson.

Buckeye quarterback Stanley Jackson threw for two touchdowns in OSU's victory over Penn State.

Germaine took his turn on the next series and didn't need a warmup, firing a 34-yard scoring pass to Stanley on the second snap.

That built a 24-0 lead and left even Cooper awestruck by the ease of OSU's ascent to 4-0 overall and 1-0 in the Big Ten.

"Was I surprised? Absolutely," Cooper said. "I thought it would be a nailbiter. Most people did."

Those expectations might have been modified had anyone known Enis would finish with 11 carries for 36 yards, well off his normal production of 6 yards per carry and 138 yards per game.

"We just weren't able to get anything going," Enis said. "It felt like they knew what plays were coming."

Even when Enis took a pitch and threw long, a play designed to penalize the town meeting OSU was staging at the scrimmage line, Kelly covered Penn State's receiver like cheese on a pizza.

"We just got licked," Paterno said. "There was nothing I could do about it. I can't even second-guess myself. It's not like I could say, 'I should have done this,' or 'I should have done that.' There's nothing I could do. We just got beat by a better football team."

After beating two top-five teams in consecutive weeks, the Buckeyes are pointing to No. 1 status.

Buckeyes Have a Rosy Future

T hey have beaten teams coached by Lou Holtz and Joe Paterno the past two weeks, and they have beaten them badly.

They have an offensive lineman, Orlando Pace, who, at 6-6 and 330 pounds, is part human being and part landslide rolling downhill. He is the best lineman this side of people named for sculleries — such as Nate "The Kitchen" Newton — who draw professional paychecks, and he will be doing that soon.

Penn State tried to confuse the Ohio State tackle by putting open space in front of him,

sending different guys at him from all angles. Pace buried them all.

When Ohio State needs yardage, the backs run behind Pace. With his bulldozer body and ballerina feet, Pace is too good for the college game. He was the best offensive lineman in the land last year as a sophomore. This year, he is the death and taxes of the game — the only certain thing. He is from Sandusky, the home of Cedar Point, and the opposing defensive coordinator each week is probably convinced he is the real Magnum.

"I'm not surprised by this," Pace said, after Ohio State destroyed Penn State, 38-7, in red and roaring Ohio Stadium yesterday. "Penn State's a little undersized. I knew we could compete with anybody in the nation. If they're No. 4 and we beat them like that after beating Notre Dame when they were No. 5, I guess we're No. 1."

ROSE-COLORED RALLY

H e was the quarterback without the magician's reputation or the miracle worker's charisma, the one from the desert who wasn't welcome in his hometown.

Joe Germaine need not go home again to be a hero, though.

He need only to board an airplane back to the Ohio State campus.

All the high esteem he could ever imagine awaits him, for the trophy Germaine grabbed yesterday as Rose Bowl MVP is only a token of the legend's status he'll forever carry in Columbus after rallying the Buckeyes to a 20-17 victory over Arizona State.

"This is a great feeling," Germaine said after finding David Boston for the winning 9-yard touchdown with 19 seconds left. "The way we did it makes it even sweeter."

The way he did it didn't sour the script either.

Not only did Germaine bounce back from being returned to backup status behind Stanley Jackson for the Rose Bowl, but Germaine, who grew up in Mesa, just a fade pattern from the Arizona State campus, also proved himself a superior rescue spe-

cialist to the Sun Devils' Jake (The Snake) Plummer yesterday.

Three years ago, when Germaine was searching for a college, ASU coach Bruce Snyder essentially told him he couldn't play for ASU because Plummer was irreplaceable.

Irreplaceable, perhaps.

But not unbeatable.

Driving OSU 65 yards to the winning score in the last 1:33, Germaine trumped the ace Plummer played when he scrambled 11 yards for a 17-14 ASU lead with 1:40 remaining.

That bit of daring seemed certain to hand Plummer his 11th fourth-quarter comeback victory in 40 career starts, but Germaine intervened.

"Joe just got the job done," Ohio State coach John Cooper said. "What a Cinderella story. The guy was raised in Mesa and apparently wasn't offered a scholarship by Arizona State, but he came back and won a big one for us today."

He won it with completion of 11, 12 and 13 yards to Dimitrious Stanley on the final drive, and two 15-yard pass interference penalties on ASU before Boston broke open.

"Football is a game of hills and valleys," said Germaine, whose 72-yard touchdown pass to Stanley at 8:23 of the third quarter overcame a 10-7

David Boston glides into the end zone with the winning score as teammate Dimitrious Stanley (3) greets him.

Ohio State split end David Boston (9) gets plenty of attention from Arizona State defenders.

ASU lead. "We knew we had the time, and we knew we had the ability to do it. We just had to get it done."

Fourth-ranked OSU finishes the season 11-1 and will aspire to its highest national ranking since a No. 2 finish following its last Rose Bowl victory in 1974.

Arizona State's (11-1) national championship hopes evaporated.

"It's tough when you think you've got it," said Plummer, who finished 19-of-35 for 201 yards. "But

BUCKEYES VS. ARIZONA STATE, 1997 ROSE BOWL

Ohio State executed the two-minute offense and won the game."

Germaine was the man for that mission, selected by Cooper to go back into the game after being replaced by Jackson the series before.

Jackson also served the Buckeyes on their first four possessions, getting them into the end zone via an 8-yard pass to Boston in the first quarter.

He gave way to Germaine early in the second quarter, though, and didn't return until the Buckeyes took control at their 3-yard line with 8:06 remaining.

Pepe Pearson flashed free on the first snap of that series and sped 62 yards to position OSU for Josh Jackson's 38-yard field-goal attempt.

Arizona State blocked the kick, and Derrick Rodgers' 50-yard touchdown return was nullified by a penalty for the forward lateral he received on the play.

Ohio State Coach John Cooper waves to his family and Buckeye friends following Ohio State's memorable victory.

No matter, for Plummer sharply marched the Sun Devils to the OSU 37, where on fourth-and-4, he lofted a textbook fade pass to Lenzie Jackson for 29 yards.

Three plays later, on third-and-11, Plummer scrambled away from pressure for the first time all afternoon, avoiding middle linebacker Andy Katzenmoyer and weaving into the end zone with a head-first flourish.

"I thought it was over right there," Katzenmoyer said. "I thought I'd blown the game."

Instead, Germaine saved it, with some help from the grab-happy Sun Devils' secondary.

"You obviously prefer a game not to end on a penalty," Snyder said. "The calls just seemed to be in the eyes of the beholder. I know it's a sensitive issue with officials, but you have to make sure it's a true infraction before you throw a flag. My point of view was it was just players battling for the football."

OSU had its own view of Ricky Boyer's 25-yard touchdown reception that pulled the Sun Devils even, 7-7.

Boyer circled wide of OSU cornerback Shawn Springs, and safety Antoine Winfield was late on arriving on the deep pattern in the end zone's left-front corner.

Winfield bumped Boyer as he adjusted, but neither that contact, nor Boyer's contact with the ground that jarred the ball into his chest, persuaded officials to throw a pass-interference flag or rule the play incomplete.

Linebacker Andy Katzenmoyer races down the sideline after an interception.

That score and Robert Nycz's 36-yard, third-quarter field goal represented the Sun Devils' only successes against OSU until Plummer rallied them to their late lead.

"Give our defense credit," Cooper said. "Any time you can hold a team that's averaging 42 points to two touchdowns, and one of them kind of questionable, you have to be proud."

Other than Germaine's long connection with Stanley, OSU's offense inspired no similar satisfaction until it mattered most.

The Buckeyes managed one first down on their three other second-half possessions until Pearson flashed up the middle and rambled deep into ASU territory, but OSU couldn't finish off

Quarterback Joe Germaine led the Buckeyes 65 yards in just 1:33 for the winning score.

the scoring opportunity.

"Without a doubt, they're the best team we've played in a long-time," Cooper said. "They put more pressure on us than we've seen in a long time."

Enough pressure to leave a bloody gash on Germaine's chin, but not enough to deny him or Ohio State.

"It was always a dream of mine to come and play in this game," Germaine said. "My dream as a kid was to do it for Arizona State. But to do it at all is just unbelievable."

Buckeyes' Victory One for the Ages

T ime had run out. Yes, after 100 of the wildest, craziest seconds, at the end of one of the wildest, craziest games the Grandaddy of Them All has ever seen.

Ohio State's Rob Kelly raised his arms and fell to his knees, like a man who had seen a vision from on high. Oh, what Ohio State had done!

Arizona State, still thrashing like a Snake with its head cut off, would get no closer than the Ohio State 35 on its last, frenzied drive. The last Sun Devils' timeout would go uncalled, because a kid named Lenzie Jackson didn't go to the ground soon enough with that last pass. A tying field goal and the certifiable madness of overtime would never happen.

At 8:35 in the East last night, the clock on the board atop the rim of the Rose Bowl read zeros across, and the score read "Ohio State 20, Arizona State 17." And all the devils, sun and otherwise, were exorcised.

Other Buckeyes were hugging, laughing and sobbing at midfield, near where the last pass had been thrown, embracing on the huge painting of a rose. Nothing would ever be so sweet again.

John Cooper, the coach who ought to have "embattled" in front of his name, had already grabbed quarterback Joe Germaine in a great, joyous bear hug. Cooper might say "cain't" and "wadn't" and "git" and kinds of other Southern expressions that come off as "bumpkinisms," but he is also the first coach to win a Rose Bowl with a Pac-10 team (with Arizona State in 1987) and a Big Ten team.

He might not win the national championship in

his 20th season as a head coach. But it took Bear Bryant and Joe Paterno 17 years to win their first; Lou Holtz 20; and Bobby Bowden, this season's favorite at Florida State, 28. Nobody will make fun of Cooper now. The monkey he got off his back could have held Fay Wray in one huge hand.

"This was for Columbus," said Cooper, as 100,635 fans looked down at the first Ohio State team in 23 years to win a Rose Bowl game.

This one was bigger than that.

This one was for every kid who ever heard Marv Homan broadcast the games of the Woody Hayes era on the radio, as he tended his chores or daydreamed his Saturdays away in a reverie of scarlet-and-gray glory.

This one was for everyone who remembers Hopalong and Archie, Horvath and Kern.

This one was for the river towns and the farmlands, for the big cities on the lake and the steel towns where the economy has gone bad.

This one was for Ohio.

It will be savored and retold, and its drama will probably redouble in the telling, although how that is possible is hard to see. The reality itself beat

almost any ending invention could devise.

With 1: 40 to play, Jake (The Snake) Plummer, the Arizona State quarterback, had flat-out stolen a game it seemed OSU could not lose. He created victory out of ashes, wriggling away from the kid assassin, freshman linebacker Andy Katzenmoyer, and zig-zagging 11 sudden yards on third-and-goal for a touchdown.

Time now for Ohio State's own cactus flower, for Germaine, the kid from suburban Phoenix, to do a little California dreamin' of his own.

Fans will talk down the years about the two third-

At one point, Arizona State had a firm grip on the Rose Bowl before the Buckeyes rallied to win.

and-longs Germaine converted with passes to Dimitrious Stanley. And about how the Sun Devils played pass defense with pitchforks and brimstone at the end, twice getting called for interference penalties. And about the little pass Germaine threw for the game-winner to a wide-open David Boston, as flustered ASU busted its coverage, with 19 seconds left.

"It doesn't get better than this," said Cooper.

Not for a long, long time.

Mountain of a Man Propels Ohio State Back to the Top

Their legend is linked arm-in-arm with the placement of a higher-profile position in the pantheon of Ohio State football greatness. Less celebrated, but no less important, obscured but not overlooked, the celebrity of the Buckeyes' greatest offensive linemen may rank a notch below that of their acclaimed running backs in prestige, but not importance. Let philosophers debate whether the chicken predates the egg or vice versa, at OSU no argument rages regarding the relationship between blocker and ballcarrier.

The tie binding those positions has never been blurred by debate over which owed its success to the other.

Instead, it has strengthened throughout a now four-decade reign marked by the respective positions feeding and flourishing from the other.

It therefore comes as no surprise to find the latest laudable OSU offensive lineman — junior tackle Orlando Pace — gaining considerable national recognition on the heels of OSU's sixth Heisman Trophy winner doing the same only a season ago.

Whether Pace made possible Eddie George's rise to prominence or whether George's school-record 1,927 rushing yards made Pace a household name isn't a new issue.

That question first came up in 1955 when Howard (Hopalong) Cassady won the Heisman with Jim Parker clearing a path up front.

Parker went on to win the first Outland Trophy the following season and finish eighth in the Heisman voting, then headed for an eight-time Pro-Bowl career with the Baltimore Colts that ended with his induction into the NFL Hall of Fame.

Nearly two decades later, Archie Griffin foreshadowed upcoming wins of the 1974 and 1975 Heismans with a fifth-place finish as a sophomore in 1973.

Ahead of Griffin that year, both on the line and in the Heisman voting, was tackle John Hicks, who nearly scored an unprecedented triple by finishing

Running back Pepe Pearson knew a good place to start a running play was behind Orlando Pace.

second in the Heisman poll while winning both the Outland and Lombardi Trophies.

Pace, then, is only the latest Buckeye blocker to both further the reputation of a talented running back and benefit from that player's success.

Parker and Hicks, though they played in different eras, consider Pace a worthy heir to the legend they helped establish.

"I've followed Ohio State football for 40 years and I like what I see out of Orlando," said Parker, who for the past 33 years has run his own pub in West Baltimore. "He's a big fellow with good speed, good balance and he really blocks well."

Hicks is closer to the current action, working for a real estate investment company in Columbus, but he sees the same things in Pace that Parker noticed.

"Orlando is a great athlete, first of all," Hicks said. "There's not much difference between the role he plays and the role I played. He's the go-to guy on that line, just like I was. You have to have a person who wants to be the guy the team goes to when the game is tough. You need that force."

Hearing those words makes a bigger impression on Pace than any opponent ever has, for while he may not be a student of OSU football history, he knows the names of the great linemen to precede him and proudly accepts their praise.

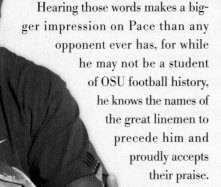

"It means a lot because those guys are the greatest offensive linemen who ever played at this school," he said. "Those guys have gone down in history. Being mentioned in the same breath with them is tremendous."

Though Parker, Hicks and Pace played roughly two decades apart and have differed in size in increasing increments — from Parker's 250 pounds, to Hicks 275 to Pace's 315 — they share several crucial commonalities that allowed them to dominate their eras.

Chief among those attributes is athleticism, which in each player's case began with the footspeed of a smaller man.

Parker, like all players in the 1950's, toiled on both sides of the scrimmage line and was as fearsome as a linebacker as he was as a blocker.

He once blocked two kicks in a high-school game and ran both back for touchdowns.

"Jim was a hell of a linebacker," said Frank (Moose) Machinski, OSU's right tackle from 1953-55. "I remember the Michigan game one year, he jumped into the line and helped us stop them on the 1-yard line.

"He was truly outstanding and one of the first really big guys to play the college game. Most of the offensive linemen in those days were 210 or 215 pounds. If you had somebody 240, he was really big.

"Jim would get on the scale and hold his hand over the weight so none of us could read it. He was listed at 230, but he was a lot bigger than that. He was just huge, and boy could he run."

Orlando Pace had an aggressive appetite at the dinner table, but still maintained his amazing foot speed.

Orlando Pace won the Rotary Lombardi Award in 1996 as the best lineman in the country.

Hicks' former teammates speak with the same reverent awe about his abilities, which helped spearhead the feared OSU option attack of the early 1970's.

"You always felt if you went John's way, it was going to be there," Griffin said. "We had that much confidence in him, and John had that much confidence in himself. John was one of those guys who'd say, 'Hey, bring it my way.'

"Not only would he tell you that, he'd tell the guy across from him that. He'd tell the defensive player before the ball was snapped, 'You bet-ter get ready, because we're coming at you.' "

Despite the warning, not many teams succeeded in stopping the Buckeyes during Hicks' junior and senior seasons, a period during which they went 19-2-1 and split a pair of lopsided Rose Bowls with USC.

"John was very, very athletic and very quick," said Fred Pagac, OSU's current defensive coordinator, who played tight end next to Hicks in 1972 and 1973. "He was huge for his day, at 275 or 280 pounds, yet he ran a 4.7.

"With size and speed like that, he was a very good base blocker. He'd just come off the ball and knock the snot out of you."

Pace, of course, specializes in that same activity, one OSU's publicity mill has given the designation, "pancakes," because of the flat state in which opponents frequently find themselves.

ORLANDO PACE: MOUNTAIN OF A MAN

"He's played his position as well as anyone else I've ever coached," OSU coach John Cooper said of Pace. "We had some great players last year — Terry Glenn, Eddie George, Bobby Hoying — but week-after-week, I don't know if we've ever had a player grade out any better than Orlando Pace.

"Last year, when he was sophomore, people didn't know a lot about him and he still won the Lombardi Trophy, the first sophomore ever to do that. I can't say for sure whether he's the best player in the country, because I haven't seen everyone play.

"But I know this, he's the best I've seen."

Coaches around the Big Ten have been of the same opinion ever since Pace walked into OSU as a freshman and became a starter from the first day of practice.

"I stood there that first day and all I could think was, 'Wow,'" said Lee Owens, Pace's first position coach, now the head coach at the University of Akron. "I mean, 'Wow, he's incredible.'

"You have to understand, I had already coached Korey Stringer, so I thought I knew a little something about offensive linemen.

"But this kid, to know everything he knew, to understand everything so well, it was absolutely remarkable."

So remarkable that Pace earned Big Ten freshman-of-the-year honors from the coaches that season, even though Indiana's Alex Smith rushed for 1,475 yards, a conference record for freshmen and the third best in NCAA Division I history for a first-year player.

"There were a lot of times as a freshman that I didn't consider myself to be a dominant player," Pace said. "It was tough at times, because I was unsure of myself. I wasn't coming off the ball like I do now.

"That started to change last year. I started to feel pretty comfortable and pretty dominant."

Pace was never more in control than in the game that probably won George the Heisman Trophy — OSU's 41-3 victory over Illinois.

The Illini swaggered into Ohio Stadium with what would prove to be the second and third players taken in the upcoming NFL draft, linebacker Kevin Hardy and defensive end Simeon Rice.

While George's OSU single-game record 314 rushing yards took the headlines that day, Pace lim-

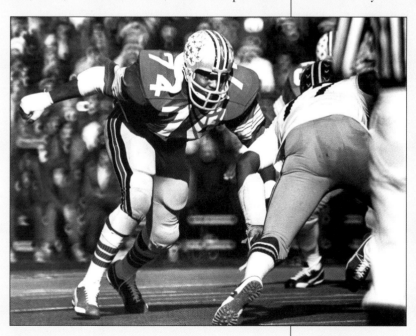

John Hicks won the Outland Trophy in 1973 as the best lineman in the country.

201

ited Rice and Hardy to seven combined tackles and zero quarterback sacks.

"In my eight seasons at Illinois, he and Tony Mandarich have been the two most dominant offensive linemen we've ever played," Illinois coach Lou Tepper said. "It's rare that an offensive lineman can make you change a game plan.

"Those are the only two since I've been in the league who've caused me, as a defensive coordinator and then as a head coach, to say, 'Wow, when we pass rush, we want to avoid him at all cost.'

"And when we go against him schematically, to say, 'Is there a way to get him over air and not a body?'"

Changes in collegiate blocking rules have allowed Pace more leeway in creating air than Parker or Hicks enjoyed during their careers.

"In those days, we had to keep our hands in," Machinski said. "If Jim could have used his hands the way they allow you to use them now, he might have had a pancake every play.

"We used to call it chicken fighting, because you had to keep your arms and push with your elbows out. You looked like a chicken doing it. Now, the whole thing is to get your hands up under the defensive player's pads to get that leverage you need to move him."

Opponents also didn't have much doubt what was coming in Parker's and Hicks' day, for Hayes was as predictable a play-caller as his legend has labeled him.

OSU tried all of 50 passes Parker's senior season of 1956, during which it rushed 524 times.

The breakdown was a bit more liberal during Hicks' final year of 1973, but not much. The Buckeyes threw 87 passes that year and rushed 728 times.

"I laugh now when I see those TV announcers talk about teams playing eight- and nine-man

fronts," Parker said. "That's all we saw back then."

"That's just the way Big Ten football was in those days," Hicks said. "Nobody threw the ball. We used to throw the hell out of it in practice, but never in the game."

The modern game demands more offensive balance, hence Pace will enter professional football with more well-rounded skills than Parker or Hicks learned at OSU.

Jim Lachey, an All-American at Ohio State in 1984 who went on to become known as the best left tackle of his era in the NFL, believes Pace "could start in the NFL right now."

"Orlando has the whole package," said Lachey, who now lives in Columbus. "He has the height, the size, the speed and the athletic ability, but most important for a great offensive lineman, he has recover ability.

"Some guys, their technique has to be perfect on every play. But Orlando can take a bad step and his feet are good enough that he can recover and still get the job done. He has everything you need."

Everything except the higher profile typically accorded quarterbacks, running backs and receivers.

"Lineman just kind of go about their business without anyone noticing," Pace said. "I got used to that a long time ago and I don't expect it to change."

The proliferation of games on television has changed some perceptions, however, otherwise Pace's Heisman Trophy candidacy wouldn't have received the serious consideration that it did.

Parker coveted the award, but knew he never had much chance of receiving it.

"When I was at Ohio State, Hopalong Cassady won it the year before I was a senior, and I knew they weren't going to give it to two Buckeyes in a row," Parker said. "I thought I was in the running for it, but I never came out and campaigned.

"You just didn't do that in those days, but I sure wanted to win it. I used to go to my room and practice my acceptance speech. My roommate, Bill Cummings, and I used to laugh about it. I had the speech ready, but they gave it to Paul Hornung (of Notre Dame).

"I thought that was the worst thing I ever heard. They didn't win but one game (actually two games) that year. I wouldn't have bothered me if Lou Michaels from Kentucky had won it, or John Brodie from Stanford. But giving it to a guy who's team was that bad, I didn't think that was right."

Hicks didn't allow himself the distraction of thinking about the Heisman, concentrating instead of returning to the Rose Bowl as a senior and avenging the 42-17 defeat Southern Cal inflicted the year before.

"That was the worst whipping any of us ever took during our careers and we promised Woody we would do something about it," Hicks said. "We dedicated that year to him.

"The honors I received that year caught me totally off guard, because in Coach Hayes' system, you didn't have individual goals. All I wanted to be was an All-America, and once I made that, I forgot about everything else.

"I remember being in a cab in New York for the Bob Hope All-American show when someone came on the radio and said (John) Cappelletti from Penn State had won the Heisman.

"Someone in the cab said, 'Who finished second?' When someone said I did, I couldn't believe it."

Pace took a philosophical view of the Heisman from the moment his campaign began.

"I can always say I got a piece of Eddie's Heisman," Pace said.

George doesn't dispute that, for he credits Pace with a big chunk of the OSU record 1,927 yards he compiled as a senior.

"Orlando is the man," George said. "He's the most amazing athlete I've ever seen on the offensive line. If you want a tough yard, just run behind Orlando. That's what we did all season."

More like every season, for the Pace/George combination is only the latest in a distinguished line of greatness that has bound OSU's ballcarriers and blockers throughout the ages.

Jim Parker cleared holes for Howard (Hopalong) Cassady.

203

Michael Wiley leaves a trail of Michigan Wolverines on his way to a 53-yard touchdown run in the first quarter of Ohio State's win in Columbus.

COOPER'S FINEST HOUR

Columbus, Nov. 21, 1998					
Michigan	0	10	3	3 –	16
Ohio State	14	7	10	0 –	31

They wanted to love him.

They really did.

Ohio State fans wanted to hug John Cooper and listen to his Southern drawl drone on and on for years to come. And they would have.

If Cooper would have just beaten Michigan, he could have talked like Mr. Ed and Buckeye fans would have threatened a pop in the mouth to anyone who made fun of Coop.

Maybe that explains why, with about 50 ticks left on the Ohio Stadium scoreboard clock, Buckeye fans could no longer hold it in. They could no longer sit back and just applaud Cooper.

In 1998, Cooper came into the final regular-season game of the year – the same one with which the Buckeyes end every season – with a miserable, painstaking, burn-him-at-the-cross 1-8-1 record against the one team every Buckeye coach has to beat: Michigan. In those eight defeats under Cooper, Ohio State lost out on five Rose Bowl invitations and squandered away four national championship runs.

This time it would be different.

Ohio State overwhelmed the Wolverines from the outset and was rewarded with a 31-16 victory. There was Cooper, standing at midfield ready to have his portrait painted. His arms crossed, his head cocked skyward taking it all in. This wasn't an everyday feeling – heck, it wasn't an every-other-year feeling – for Cooper. He tasted the joy of becoming a father more often than that of beating Michigan.

Running back Michael Wiley got the scoring started on Ohio State's second possession. He broke a 53-yard touchdown run through a large hole provided by fullback Matt Keller. Wiley slashed past defenders and then brushed off a Michigan defender at the 45 to clear daylight and a 7-0 lead.

On the ensuing possession, Michigan's fate was doomed. Punter Jason Vinson needed to have a good day against the Buckeyes' punt-return team – named the "score unit" all season – and he did not. Ohio State pressured Vinson, who mishandled the snap, and Michigan set up the Buckeyes at the Wolverine 16 thanks to a negative-yardage punt.

Shortly after, quarterback Joe Germaine hit Dee Miller for a 14-0 lead.

Before halftime, Vinson would watch as Ohio State blocked a punt. That led to a Germaine–to–David Boston score. Suddenly the 94,339 people were rocking the Olentangy River.

"You could see it in our eyes that we were going to have a big game," Germaine said.

Off to the side, Ohio State tucked away its recruits. One of the players standing on the sideline that day was Mike Doss. He would commit to Ohio State and four years later be a part of the biggest game in Ohio State history.

Cooper, however, would not.

When the final seconds ticked, Cooper was lost in a sea of scarlet and gray; some of the very same fans who had blistered him on talk radio now hugged the coach who tore the albatross off his collar – if only for the second (and last) time.

This was their coach, and dagummit, they loved him for the final time.

Ohio State's David Boston pulls in a first-quarter pass in front of Michigan's Tommy Hendricks during the Buckeyes' 31-16 victory in Columbus in 1998.

A RALLYING CRY

They sat stone-cold quietly in a locker room looking at nothing but the walls and each other. A few minutes had passed since South Carolina kicker Daniel Weaver reached through their chests and pulled their hearts out.

This was defeat and pain, and it was the starting point for the incredible run the Buckeyes would have toward the 2002 national championship. Nothing worth working hard for ever started without pain.

Ohio State had just lost a heartbreaking 31-28 Outback Bowl game against South Carolina to finish the 2001 season. It was the same place where they had embarrassed themselves a year earlier. But somehow this wasn't the same as the 24-7 Outback Bowl loss to South Carolina following the 2000 season.

In that one, everything seemed to revolve around the happenings off the field. In his final week as head coach, John Cooper watched his program crumble from the inside. Two players fought, and one ended up suing the other. Another player had a grade-point average of 0.0. This wasn't a team as much as it was a gathering of individuals.

Until Jim Tressel took over.

In his first season, 2001, he steered Ohio State to a win over Michigan and another berth in the Outback Bowl. He watched stoically in the first half as his team dug a 21-0 hole. There was nothing he could do in the third quarter when South Carolina took a 28-0 lead, and television sets around Ohio were turned off.

But Ohio State rose from the ashes on this sunny January day in Florida. Buckeye quarterback Steve Bellisari, himself embarrassed by an arrest for driving under the influence about a month earlier, took it upon his shoulders to play with respect and heart in his last game wearing scarlet and gray. Bellisari led Ohio State to a comeback as he completed 21-of-35 passes for 320 yards. He scored on a 2-yard run as the clock ticked down to end the third quarter.

The run for the Fiesta Bowl a year later started here. It began when Bellisari connected with tight end Darnell Sanders for a 16-yard score early in the fourth. It continued when Jonathan Wells ran over a defender on his way to the end zone from a yard out with 5:02 to play.

With less than two minutes to play, Sanders hauled in a 9-yard pass from Bellisari to tie the game. The Ohio State sideline celebrated its comeback, both on this day and in so many other ways.

But there was Weaver, ready to stick a pin in their balloon. He lined up for a 42-yard field goal. Ohio State coaches made sure freshman safety Dustin Fox was on the field. He is the team's best leaper. Weaver's kick started low over the line of

Tampa, Fla., Jan., 1, 2002					
So. Carolina	0	14	14	3	31
Ohio State	0	0	7	21	28

scrimmage.

The difference between defeat and overtime was inches. "I could feel the breeze of the ball as it passed over my hand," Fox said.

The ball made it over the crossbar the same way a car floats into a gas station on fumes. Ohio State had lost, but it made the Buckeyes a team.

"What we did (in the 2002 season) started at the end of the Outback Bowl," tight end Ben Hartstock said a week before Ohio State won the national championship over Miami.

"There was a pact made among the players who were part of the Ohio State family," said three-time All-American safety Mike Doss. "None of us ever wanted to feel like that again after a game. It was awful, the worst feeling you can imagine. We were so close to winning that game, and to lose it like that.... Time expires, (the ball is) almost blocked, and then barely makes it over the crossbar. We remember what it felt like in that locker room before we started."

The next time the Buckeyes would take the field, they would have a bond. They had shed blood and tears together and came up short. Not anymore.

After losing in the Outback Bowl to end the 2001

season, Ohio State would play the 2002 season without a loss. The Buckeyes would win 14 straight games and pull off one of the biggest upsets in college football history over Miami.

But it started against South Carolina.

Michael Doss takes down South Carolina quarterback Phil Petty during the Buckeyes' 31-28 Outback Bowl loss in Tampa.

FINDING A WAY TO WIN

It was not designed to be the play that saved the season. It was just supposed to be the play that saved the second.

With about 100 seconds left on a chilly late fall day, Jim Tressel sent the play in from the sideline. Ohio State was trailing 6-3 and had a fourth-and-1 at the Purdue 37-yard line. This is what it came down to: a 10-0 record and the No. 3 ranking in the country were on the line with 1:40 to play.

Tressel made the call: "King right, 64 shallow swat."

Ohio State's offense hurried to the line, opting to save their two remaining timeouts. Quarterback Craig Krenzel looked over the defense; the same brain that aces biochemistry exams in the classroom analyzed what he now had before him.

Purdue, naturally, thought run. With Maurice Clarett on the sideline after reaggravating a season-long shoulder injury, Ohio State had Maurice Hall in the backfield. Who would have thought that Clarett was a decoy on the biggest play of the season so far?

The Boilermaker cornerbacks were rolled up in man-to-man press coverage, without a safety deep. Tressel, who played most games during the season with the top button on his shirts tightened, surely wouldn't roll the dice and go deep here, would he?

No, he wouldn't. Krenzel would.

The first read on the play was tight end Ben Hart-stock, whose route took him on a short pattern in the left flat. Hartstock should have received the safe pass, a safe call designed to keep the chains moving. But Purdue jumped Hartstock.

Krenzel noticed big-play wide receiver Michael Jenkins breaking open and getting a step on the coverage down the left sideline, just beyond Hartstock. Jenkins adjusted his post route and ran past cornerback Antwaun Rogers. Krenzel stepped up in the pocket, partly to avoid slight pressure, partly to allow Jenkins more time to put some separation between himself and Rogers.

Krenzel let loose with the pass, a ball that seemed to hang in the air for minutes. There was more than air riding on that ball. Every ounce of hope for a national title twirled in the wind with the spiral. The pass fell over Jenkins' shoulders and into his soft hands in the end zone for a touchdown and a

West Lafayette, Ind., Nov. 9, 2002					
Ohio State	0	3	0	7 —	10
Purdue	3	0	0	3 —	6

10-6 Buckeyes victory. Ohio State had another improbable comeback and side stepped a land mine on the way toward the Fiesta Bowl.

"That was our season in a nutshell, right there," Hartstock said. "An entire year's worth of preparation and practice came down to that moment."

As soon as Jenkins caught the ball, Krenzel raised both arms in the air in celebration. "You don't have time to think, 'Hey, this is the season,'" Krenzel said. "All you're thinking about is, 'It's fourth down and we need this many yards for a first down.'"

It would not be the last time Krenzel saved the Buckeyes with a fourth-down pass during the 2002 season.

A key point in the game was lost in the excitement of the fourth-and-1 touchdown pass. Late in the second quarter, linebacker Matt Wilhelm picked off a Boilermaker pass at the Purdue 41. Ohio State drove down the field, inside the 10.

Twice during that drive, Krenzel said to hell with throwing the football and took off on his feet. He gained 22 yards on those runs.

With no timeouts and the clock ticking away, the Buckeyes sent place-kicker Mike Nugent on to the field. The field-goal unit hurried to their positions and the ball was snapped just before the scoreboard clock hit 0:00. Nugent made a 22-yard field goal and Ohio State tied the game at 3-3.

Krenzel finished the game with a rather humble stat line: 13-of-20 completions for 173 yards. But those numbers don't do justice to this quarterback's personality: calm, cool, collected, and cerebral.

"Panic is not a part of our vocabulary," defensive end Simon Frasier said. "There's a belief that we will win the game."

Ohio State coach Jim Tressel calls for a one-point conversion following the Buckeyes' only touchdown of the Purdue game on Nov. 9, 2002, in West Lafayette, Ind.

UNBEATEN, UNTIED, UNSTOPPABLE

Columbus, Nov. 23, 2002

Michigan	3	6	0	0	– 9
Ohio State	7	0	0	7	– 14

In Ohio, a state infamous for Red Right 88, the Drive, the Fumble, blowing Game 7 of the 1997 World Series, Mike Brown, and the Bengals, fans have come to expect disappointment.

Especially in big games.

The last time Ohio State beat Michigan at home was 1998. No one could really blame Ohio State fans if they expected Michigan quarterback John Navarre to somehow, some way, find the end zone as the final seconds left the clock with the Buckeyes clutching at a 14-9 lead.

On the Buckeye sideline just before the last snap of the game, three Ohio State University police officers surrounded head coach Jim Tressel. One stood on each side, and the third behind him. In the Ohio State end zone, the Buckeyes surrounded Navarre's pass.

Mike Doss, Will Allen, and Donnie Nickey engulfed the pass, the prayer that was thrown after one second remained and Navarre took the snap from the Buckeyes' 21.

For a brief few seconds, 105,539 fans at Ohio Stadium gasped. The ball was on the way to the end zone. Everything rode on this play: a 13-0 record, a trip to the national title game in the Fiesta Bowl, a share of the Big Ten championship, and a helluva lot of pride.

SWAT. Allen's right hand came in and he was able to get two hands on the ball to intercept the pass and secure the win.

Doss, a three-time All-American who had announced that he would return for his senior season because he wanted to win a national title, fell to the ground on his knees. Tears fell from his face.

Ohio State 14, Michigan 9.

The Buckeyes won this game with hard work and a never-quit attitude. Michigan moved the ball up and down the field in the first half, but had only three field goals to show for their work.

"They had nine points and 200 yards on us at the half," Doss said. "I told our defense, 'That's not the way our defense plays.' We just decided in the next 30 minutes to leave it all out there on the field. We played as a unit, and when it was time to make a stop, we made it."

There was no other way to end the regular season. The Buckeyes made the fans' hearts stop nearly each week of the season.

"I guess, it's our calling card," said tight end Ben Hartstock.

The record crowd stormed the field even though

officers had been stationed around the stadium to keep them off. The goalposts had been greased to make it nearly impossible for fans to rip them from the ground.

At one entrance point, a police officer was seen helping fans over a railing to celebrate on the field. Laws? Who cared. Ohio State was heading to the national championship game for the first time since 1968.

"It's a dream come true to get to this point," linebacker Matt Wilhelm said. "Obviously we have one game, one huge game, left. We've attained some of the goals we've talked about this season, but the big one is still left."

Freshman running back Maurice Clarett finished with 119 yards on the ground. More importantly, Clarett hauled in a 26-yard pass from quarterback Craig Krenzel down the left sideline to the Michigan 6.

How important was Clarett against Michigan? He averaged 7 yards each time he touched the ball, even though he was nursing an injured shoulder throughout the game. Tressel was forced to rest him at times. At those times, the Buckeyes managed less than 4.5 yards.

Ohio State quarterback Craig Krenzel breaks free from Michigan's Larry Stevens for a 5-yard gain in the fourth quarter in Columbus.

The go-ahead score came when Krenzel took the snap and ran an option pitch to running back Maurice Hall. The Buckeyes had practiced the quarterback option all season, and tore the yellowed page out of the playbook for this one play.

Hall scored. The house was rocking.

When the game was over, and the torn-up field finally cleared, all that remained were remnants of a wild celebration. The debris was collected in the scoreboard end zone. A few fans lost a shoe – just one, not a pair. God help the poor soul who was looking for his asthma inhaler during the melee.

A woman's bra, somehow, didn't look out of place.

The smell of pepper spray never tasted so sweet. Police sprayed a small area of the field to try to control the crowd. Maybe it worked. The goal posts remained in the ground.

"In a way, we were never able to see the big picture because we focused on each of the last 13 weeks," said defensive tackle Kenny Peterson. "When my adrenaline settles down, this will sink in."

DARING TO DREAM

They said it couldn't be done. They said a team that won six games by a touchdown or less, and trailed in their final four games, was lucky to be there. They said Ohio State, a two-touchdown underdog against Miami, with college football's longest current winning streak at 34 games, could not beat the Hurricanes.

Lucky? Sure.

They were also the best team – yes, *team* – in the country.

After two overtimes, a premature celebration caused by a flag thrown late, and a heart-stopping fourth-and-long pass completion, the Buckeyes did what just about nobody thought they would do before the 2002 season started.

For the first time since 1968, Ohio State was consensus national champion, and they did it the same way as Woody did it in '68: with a head coach who called the oh-so-right play for a team that believed it was a band of brothers.

"I hope what they get from this is what it takes to be champions," Tressel said. "All of the people who are important, all of the things that they have done, and all of the lessons learned – if they get that, I don't care if they ever get what it means to be national champions. I hope they get the lessons."

At the end of the first overtime, it looked and sounded like Ohio State's national title dreams had fallen short. A fourth-down pass fell incomplete in the end zone at the end of the first overtime. Miami players celebrated, some by throwing their helmets in the air. Fireworks danced against the evening Arizona sky.

Buckeye quarterback Craig Krenzel looked on from the ground, tears starting to fill his eyes.

"I was stunned," cornerback Dustin Fox said. "I couldn't believe we had lost."

Had they? Was the game really over?

"I already had tears in my eyes," Fox said. "I mean, the game was over. Miami rushed the field, the fireworks went off. It was like a miracle."

Like?

One referee was replaying the last play over and over in his head. He wanted to get the call right. So Terry Porter threw the "flag heard 'round the world." Miami freshman Glenn Sharpe and Ohio State intended receiver Chris Gamble were entangled shortly before the pass arrived. Porter called pass interference.

Ohio State lived.

"I fell to my knees," running back Lydell Ross said. "Then I heard the announcer say, 'Wait a minute. There's a flag on the field.'"

Of course, that play never would have happened had it not been for an even more dramatic play just

Quarterback Craig Krenzel celebrates his touchdown, which tied the Fiesta Bowl and sent it into double overtime, where the Buckeyes finally prevailed 31-24 over Miami.

Tempe, Ariz., Jan. 3, 2003						
Ohio State	0	14	3	0	14	–	31
Miami	7	0	7	3	7	–	24

before the flag in the end zone. Ohio State had fourth-and-14, which might as well have been fourth-and-Phoenix, earlier in the first overtime. Krenzel dropped back to pass. He threw for Michael Jenkins along the right sideline. Jenkins toed the out of bounds strip and hauled in the 17-yard pass for a first down.

A few moments later, in the second overtime, Ohio State dealt Miami its own dose of fourth-down heartache. Ohio State's offense was on the field for the second possession of the first overtime period. That meant the Buckeyes would get the ball to start the second over-time with the game tied at 24.

It also meant Miami's defense would be on the field for the two possessions. They breathed heavily as Ohio State huffed and puffed the ball down their throats. Fresh-man running back Maurice Clarett took over and bull-rushed his way over the Miami defensive for the go-ahead score.

Ohio State Coach Jim Tressel holds up the championship trophy after the Buckeyes beat Miami 31-24 in two overtimes in the Fiesta Bowl on Jan. 3, 2003, in Tempe, Ariz.

The Hurricanes would try to send it to a third overtime. Miami had fourth-and-goal from the 2. The call from the sideline was "Tight Will Tulsa." It had weak-side linebacker Cie Grant's name written all over it.

"You know what that means," Grant said. "It means Cie Grant is coming off the edge, and I'm bringing the juice. It's do-or-die time."

Seconds after Ken Dorsey took the shotgun snap, Grant had the All-American quarterback, who was famous for leading his team to last-minute come-backs and winning 34 straight games, wrapped up. He flung the ball toward no one in particular. It was batted down in the end zone by Donnie Nickey.

A few weeks later, with sixty thousand Ohio State fans braving temperatures that dipped into the single digits back in Columbus, the Buckeyes celebrated their first Bowl Championship Series national title.

Their moment had been defined. The greatest team in every sense of the word was able to enjoy the greatest moment in Ohio State football.

"There are hundreds of memories I can give you from what we went through this season," senior defensive tackle Kenny Peterson said. "The one memory I'm going to take away from this is the memories I had with the other players and coaches. I'm going to remember sticking my facemask in theirs before the Fiesta Bowl and saying, 'C'mon, let's go.' It almost brings tears to my eyes to realize I can't do that anymore.... It doesn't really hit you until you realize the Fiesta Bowl was our last time together."